HARM'S WAY

The fight we almost lost

by MARILYN M. JENNINGS

TO:_______________________________

FROM:_____________________________

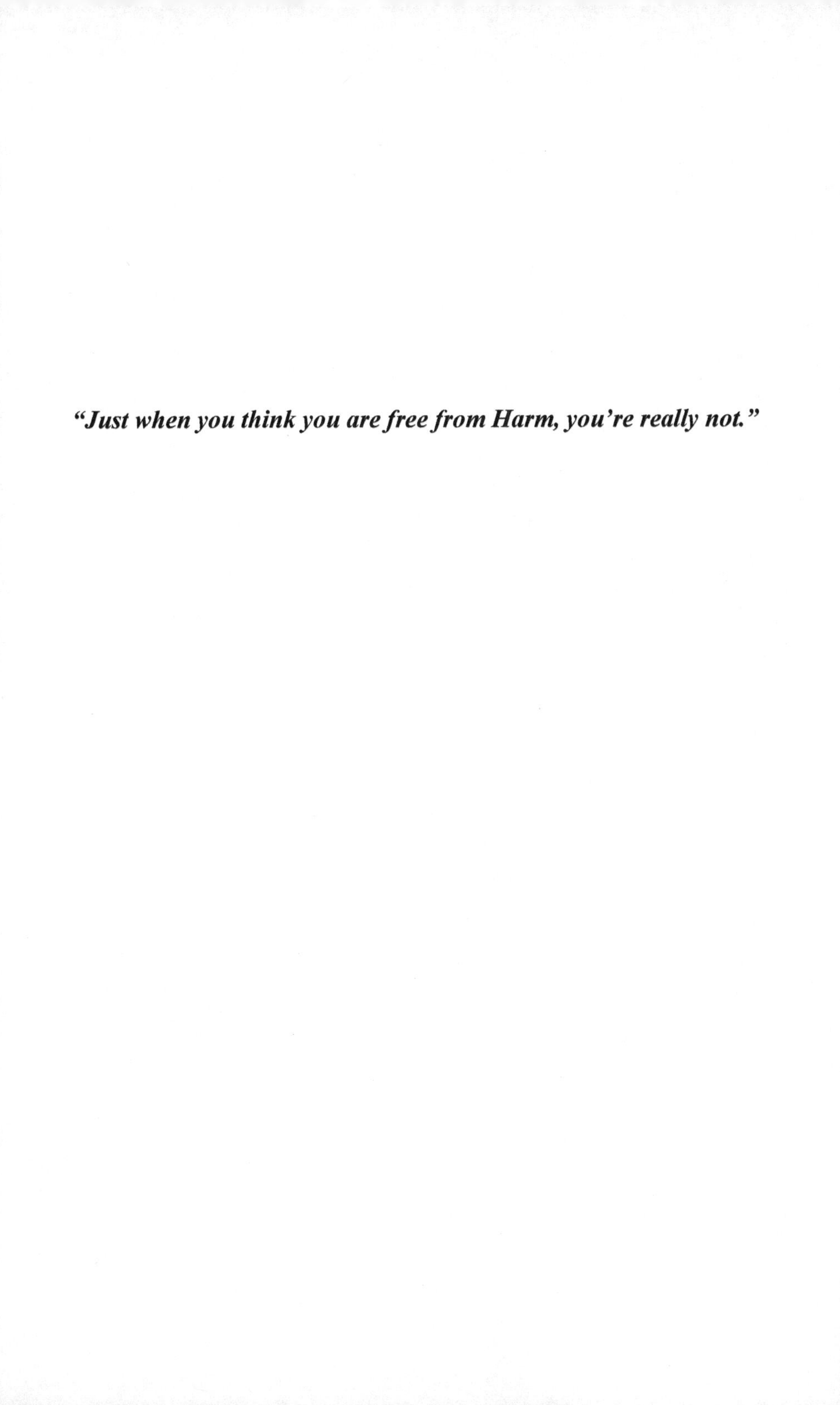

"Just when you think you are free from Harm, you're really not."

HARM'S WAY

THE FIGHT WE ALMOST LOST

MARILYN M. JENNINGS

Harm's Ways: The Fight We Almost Lost

ISBN 978-0-692-09897-4

For information contact HarmsWayCv@Gmail.com

Cover Design & Book Layout by: Kantis Simmons
Book Editor: Tiffany Poole
The SIMAKAN Group.

Warning - Disclaimer

FOREWORD

Walking toward the track of a local middle school in Jonesboro, GA for a walk sponsored by My Sister's Keeper, we never knew what an impactful walk we were about to takein 2009. My husband, Rev. Richard Jones, had been asked to come out and support our churchmate, Marilyn Jennings,and to offer up a prayer for the group's cause.

After walking a few laps, the entire group gathered around for prayer and Marilyn began to share her story. She was so statuesquebut stood with her neck held down. A heart-wrenching recollection spilled out, and it was then we realized it was her beautiful 24-year-old sister who was gunned down in 2007 at the CNN Center, making national news. We still vividly remembered the shock and public outcry. The Ladies of My Sister's Keeper members knew the story all too well, but none could contain their tears as they listened and reflected on their own domestic violence stories.We too could not hold back our tears as Richard prayed over each of them. Our lives changed forever as our relationship has blossomed into a godparent/brother-sisterhoodand as we sought to help her on her journey since that day.

This book, "Harm's Way," was birthed out of the bottomless pain of that day in 2007 and from Marilyn's great determination to tell the story of Clara Riddles. In becoming Clara's Voice, we have watched Marilyn grow in grace and boldness in representing the voices of many domestic violence victims and survivors, even as she sheds light on her own personal victimization. With the creation of her own non-profit organization Harm's Way Inc. and becoming a community activist, we pray many continued blessings on the life of Marilyn Jennings to keep up this necessary work.

To all who read this book, may the grace of God and the communion of his Holy Spirit heal, comfort and strengthen your life if you are touched in any way by the words in this book and by the devastating issue of domestic violence.

- Rev. Richard and Valerie Jones

All praises are due to Marilyn Jennings, for bringing the awareness of Domestic Violence to the forefront. Knowing it hits so close to home for her, this book will allow many victims to identify, as well speak out, about their own experiences stemming from Domestic abuse. No matter if its physical, verbal, or even physiological, no one should have to deal with the effects which lingers and keeps them sheltered inside. Harm's Way Book and foundation will be the voice, to allow people who's been affected to speak out, in order for the healing process to begin. This book is a constant page turner, to help refine the inner substance, which is needed. Again I say all praises due to the author.

- Fernando Settles

INSPIRATION

The day we met was a day of preparation. I still remember how we went from having a professional meeting about how our respective programs could collaborate to serve seniors, and ended up in a deeply personal conversation about life, love and loss. HE was preparing us.

As a social worker and public administrator, my role has always been one that moved from attention (listening to a person's story) to advocacy (using my gifts, talents and abilities) to help in any way that I could.

Clara's story, coupled with your unwavering dedication to be a raging voice against Domestic Violence, moved me in such a way that I eagerly embraced the thought of serving as a soldier in Clara's army. I was there to praise, encourage, guide and even challenge you to go to the next level in your God-given mission. HE was preparing you.

Little did I know, thirty days later I would be faced with the murder of my younger sister, Patrice Bryant. HE was preparing me. I thank God everyday for bringing your light into my life, and I am so proud of how you have stepped into your mission and will be the voice of not only, Clara, but Patrice and the countless others, who have lost their lives to the dreaded (and unnecessary) disease of Domestic Violence.

This book will serve as a cautionary tale of how cycles are perpetuated (even when we are not aware of doing so). More importantly, it will serve as a supportive guide to help victims, survivors, and families break the chains of Domestic Violence......and find their voice. HE is preparing them. I salute you, my sister and dear friend, for being the voice and having NO TIME FOR IT!

Peace & Blessings,

Partrounar Bryant-James

DEDICATION

The two hardest things I had to do in my life was burying my sister Clara and writing this book.

There was nothing in life that could have prepared me for the day that I lost her. It took a lot of prayer and willpower to not only overcome her death, but to want to raise awareness because of it. I not only want to fight this deadly killer, I want to win. I want to save lives.

There are so many people who have experienced the loss of someone to domestic violence and are wondering what happened and why they didn't see the signs.

What if I was to say the signs were there but you were just not paying attention?

Clara's death taught me so many things. I am more focused on the signs of domestic violence than I ever have been. I can see all the signs that I ignored before. There is not one day that goes by that I do not think about her. I ponder often what life would be like if she was still here with us.

I know that God has a purpose behind everything and I trust and know that He is in control of it all.

For my sister and others who have lost their lives to domestic violence and those who are survivors and are still trying to get out or don't believe they can get out; you have a voice that hears your call.

Along with others, we will raise awareness in our communities, cities, states, and country. We are going to win our lives back. We are going to change the mindset of those that give domestic violence power. And we are going to help people get away to safety so that they don't have to be another voice lost.

Forever a voice

#bethevoice

TABLE OF CONTENTS

INTRODUCTION

I never thought that I would be writing a book explaining things that I have encountered throughout my life. I am a survivor of many things. My life hasn't been "a walk in the park". I am pretty sure there are a lot of us that think the same way.

I kept most of my struggles hidden within hoping that one day I will simply forget about them or have enough distraction in life so I can just ignore them. This would also be the reason why some people don't find healing and carry their burdens and disappointment through one generation after the next. I'm pretty sure most of us think like that.

Well, I am here to let you know that until you face that very thing that tore you down, it will always have the ability to detour your current situation at any given time. In order to heal from broken areas in your life, you must first identify what broke you in the first place.

****

PURPOSE

The reason for me writing this book is very simple. I had to write it. It wasn't something that I always wanted to do. When the time came, I knew our story had to be told.

My sister gave me the title of this book because of the last song she sang to me: "Because of love you placed yourself in harm's way". These were some of the words that run through my mind whenever I think of her. When she was killed I was devastated because I truly thought we would survive living under the roof of domestic violence. I was able to protect her when we were kids but I couldn't protect her as an adult; a pain that I carry every day. "I truly do believe that if I was there when she was killed, because of love, I would have prevented her death -even if it meant sacrificing my life. But God saw fit to keep me here to tell the story.

Clara would always ask, "Why do you care so much?" And later she sang those same words to me: "Because of love you placed yourself in harm's way." Some days I can still hear her singing. Clara, sing my sister. Sing. I know that if I would have been with her on the day she lost her life I wouldn't be here writing this book.

So, in return, and because of my love, I tell our story to hopefully speak to someone who is going through or thought they have survived domestic violence.

I hope that my book will enlighten you on what we missed and how domestic violence is able to come in quietly and destroy everything in its path. When you think you are free from harm, you are really not.

Chapter 1

MY Life Matters

Well, Mom decides not to let me go to work today. "Come home straight from school," she said. We were having family problems and she wanted to talk about them. She was fed up with my attitude and wanted to address the issues. I have not been speaking to my dad for a couple of weeks now and I wasn't going to ever again. Days of him drinking and making us stand at attention, the constant name-calling and the unnecessary beatings were no more for me -- I QUIT!!!! Putting up with his bullshit was too much for me and I wanted out, even if it meant leaving home at an early age. I was fifteen, in the 11th grade, and all I wanted to do was to graduate, but instead, I had to fight for my purpose.

My parents met when I was three months. My mother was thirteen and my father was seventeen. I grew up not knowing my biological father. My stepfather has been the only father figure I ever knew. To me he is dad.

Dad stood about 5'10 with a slender built, very tone small frame. He was dark skin with reddish like pupils, probably because he drunk a lot. He was in his 30s. His demeanor was very cold and scary. We would be nervous every time he came home He didn't smile much and didn't have a lot to say until he was under the influences of alcohol. Dad had a hard deep thunderous voice that whenever he called one of our names, and adrenaline rush would be there as went hurried to him hoping that we didn't do anything wrong. He was very strict and didn't play around with us at all. He loved to get in our face with that alcohol breath and those bad teeth. His front teeth were brown and rotten. He ate almost everything and never complain about having toothache. I personally think from all the alcohol he drunk his gums were numb to pain.

He was a very neat dresser. The majority of his clothes went to the cleaners. All of his jeans had to be heavy starch. He would get dress in his nice clothes just to sit around the house watching television and drinking. We could always count on dad to buy us something nice every now and then if we asked. Birthdays were always the best time to ask for an outfit that we probably wouldn't get any other time.

Once he was intoxicated he would want to drive to go get more to drink and ask me to ride with him. Sometimes he would be so drunk that he would try to get me to drive him home. " Now that was funny because I didn't know the first thing about driving but there I was behind the wheel barley pushing the gas pedal, trying to stay in my lane on a two lane road. Luckily we were not that far from home. Then there were times he would just sit in a room and cry reminiscing about people whom have gone on to glory, mainly his mother. Always repeating his stories over and over until he fell asleep.

Dad wasn't the father that we could hug and play with like other kids could. But Every night before we went to bed we would give them a kiss on the check and say goodnight, that was something that we was taught as kids, and to always say good morning.

Mom, was high yellow, slightly heavy set. She was maybe 5'7 in height. Mom had thick beautiful yellow legs that would always get attention when she showed them. She didn't wear a lot of makeup. Sometimes she would put on a little dark red lipstick. She stuttered some when she talked. A lot more when she was upset or overly excited. Mom was very easy going at times but would explode out of control when we made her mad. She worked a lot and cooked almost every day to make sure we had hot meals. She was good at putting meals together even when there was very little to eat in the house. Mom was very passive with a lot of the things that happen in the house. Dad was loud and abusive verbally and physically to mom and she would just cry some and pretend like everything was okay. She tried very hard to please my father and he would always seem to be unappreciative of everything she tried to do for him. Mom was a strong, determined women that was trying to raise us to the best of her abilities. Always teaching us morals and having respect for others. Mom didn't go out much. She didn't have many friends and kept to herself most of the times. She was a very private person. No one knew the abuse she suffered and she never plan on talking about it to anyone. When she was not working she was at home making sure all the things around the house were did. Most of her money went on bills, and keeping my father out of jail. There were times when she could not get my father out of jail so mom had to work extra jobs to keep a roof over our head and food in our bellies until he got out to help her. She wouldn't tell anyone that my dad was in jail. No matter how long he would be incarcerated for drinking and driving or for disorderly conduct.

Through the years I saw how my dad's constant abuse weaken her mentally and physically. Little did she know I was watching how the glow she once had withered away due to her enduring all the verbalizing torture from my father and I knew at a young age I didn't want that for myself. I admire mom in so many ways but I was so disappointed to see her get depress and sometimes suicidal, over my father, when she could of just left him and started over. Quitting was not an option for my mom and she was willing to do and accept things they way they were in order to keep her family as one.

Mom said that she was not going to work that night, but she lied. When I got home, Clara was there waiting on me, as usual. She ran to me every time I came through the door. We slept in the same room and shared the same bed. She was three years old. She was my little sister that God had created for me. I felt obligated to protect her and keep her safe from any harm or danger. My younger brother Thadd had come home with some friends and they were in the living room playing with their toys. It was cold and raining outside, so everyone had to stay in.

Mom had left instructions for me to cook dinner; she had taken out some chicken that she wanted me to fry in the deep fryer. Dad had been drinking, so I knew things were not going to go well. He had so many personalities that only came out when he was drinking and he always revealed every last one of them to me. I hated him so much. When he drank, it would always remind me he was not my father. Hell, that didn't matter to me. Shit, as mean as he was, I didn't care at all. Honestly, it hurt every time he said it. I remember meeting my biological father when I was maybe six or seven. It was in the summer of 1979. My brother and I were visiting grandmother for the summer. I was already in bed when there was a knock on the front door. A few minutes later, I was awakened by my grandmother and was told that someone wanted to meet me. As I walked to the living room with my eyes barely open, I can see a man, lady, and a little girl around my age all staring at me. The man told me he was my father and that he was in town and wanted to meet me. I didn't say much; I just stood there very nervous. I didn't know what to say. If I said anything I don't remember, it was so long ago. I don't even remember his name. I went back to bed. I slept on a rollaway that my grandmother had in her room. Within a few min the man and his family came to my room. He called out my name, but I didn't answer. I was scared so I pretended to be sleep. He put some money in my hands and then they left. I never saw him again. Throughout my life I would have moments wondering if I was dreaming, or if it was real, and wondering too why he never tried to see me again, and where was when I needed him. I felt as though I didn't belong anywhere.

Doing as I was told, I went into the kitchen to fry the chicken.

My father came behind me and stood there looking. He started saying that I was a lot of trouble and that he was tired of me messing up his family. Here we go. Why me? I said to myself. How are you going to blame me for your drinking problems? He would wake us up in the middle of the night fussing about anything. We would watch him fight our mom and we couldn't do anything about it. She would cry and tell us that everything would be okay. I knew she was lying. My brother and I would get up the next morning and fix the mess that he made -- pick up all the broken glass, throw away all the flower pots and put all the food that we could save back in the refrigerator. He would be asleep in their room and wouldn't remember anything he did. And Mom would accept his excuse. I said to myself, "So I'm to blame for standing up for myself!" I had been called so many bitches and whores, that I didn't care about no one but my sister, for I was going to make sure that she was safe. I was 14 at the time and my brother had just turned 13 and I didn't know what I was going to do. All I knew was enough was enough! Direction, I didn't have any; not even a clue how I was going to handle my troubles. The burden in my heart was heavy, my stomach was in knots. The hurt and anger that I was feeling gave me the only courage I had to fight back with. I knew I wasn't going to win; I just wasn't ready to idly live or die like this.

My dad wasn't a walk in the park, but he tried to love us the best way he knew how. He talked a lot when he was drinking and would tell us stories of his childhood.

As a little boy living in New Jersey, he had to help out around the house a lot, especially with his little brother and sisters because his mother was sick with cancer and his father wasn't around. He was the oldest of four siblings. His mom gave him the nickname "Fly" because he could run very fast. He grew up in the projects, and when she sent him to the store he would run fast so the kids couldn't catch him and take his money. He would break out in laughter every time he told that story.

His mom died when he was just 13 and that changed his life forever. She promised him that the surgery she was preparing to have would be her last surgery and she would be okay after that. My father's mother died during that surgery so she wasn't able to keep her promise. In some sort of way, I believe that my father was mad and hurt behind that promise because he would never make a promise to us. He would always say he would try but he never would promise.

We would sit up for hours talking about his childhood and how he dropped out of school. He would tell us to not make the same mistakes he made and that it was important that we got an education.

He stressed that he wanted us to do better than him. I promised him I would and he told me he was going hold me to that. It was important to him that we got our education because he didn't want us to struggle through life the way he and my mother did. I said I was going to be a lawyer and take care of my parents.

They worked hard, long hours but seemed to not make enough to keep the bills paid. We went through a lot of hardship but Mom knew how to make our bellies full even when the kitchen cabinets were bare. We lived by some very strict rules and very harsh punishments, but we still managed to find time to laugh. Watching my parents fight and struggle, I knew I wanted to have a better life for myself. They wanted that for us as well but just didn't know how to help us get there. They were young trying to raise children.

There in the kitchen, I had just taken out the first batch of chicken. My father tells me that he should put my head in the deep fryer and that would solve their entire problems. He said that I was disrupting his family. I was just causing too many problems. He said he could just kill me and everything would be over. No one would miss me, he said. He said he would tell them I just ran away again and no one would care. I believed him; he had already done awful things to me before so I knew he was serious.

Without him noticing, I slowly turned off the deep fryer. I gave him an excuse to walk out of the kitchen. I told him that I was going to change my clothes, and he followed. He even told my brother and his friends to follow him to my room. "Do y'all want to see somebody naked?" he yelled. My room door was locked but he was trying to break it in. He pressed hard on my room door trying to get in. I pressed my bodyweight against the door, trying to hold them off. I stood behind the door only taking off the shirt leaving my t-shirt and overalls on at the time. I opened the door and came out into the living room to sit down. I was too afraid to go back into the kitchen. He walked to his room and waited. When he returned he told my brother's friends they had to leave. He was angry and I knew that I was to blame. He went to the kitchen to grab a piece of chicken. He walked back to the living room where I was sitting. "Chicken was good," he said to me. "Marilyn, go back into the kitchen and finish cooking dinner." I said nothing. I didn't even move. I was scared shitless because I never disobeyed my father, but I wasn't going back in that kitchen. He told me again. He realized that I wasn't obeying him so he got mad. He yelled at me again, stating that if I didn't get off my ass and do as I was told he was going to slap the shit out of me. I had to be out of it because I was so afraid of my father, I never saw myself disobeying anything he said. His voice would make us jump every time he called our name, and we hoped that we hadn't done anything wrong when we answered his call.

He would remember promises of punishment that he would bring up at any given time. We never knew what to expect when he called, and I always inhaled even when he just wanted something from the kitchen. It was always best for me to do what my father asked because my brother would always get it wrong. The glass would be dirty or the fork wasn't cleaned properly. I knew how to check to make sure everything was perfect before I brought anything to my father. We would rotate the cleaning of my parents' room on Saturday and my brother would beg me to switch with him so he wouldn't get yelled at for not cleaning their room properly. I would agree because I knew how to clean my parents' room and clean the mirrors in the bathroom without leaving streaks on the mirror.

On that day I wasn't trying to please him. I no longer looked at him as my father but as the man that had been mistreating me for a long time and I was ready for a change. I took a deep breath and grabbed the end of the chair to brace myself because I knew he was going to do what he just said. He told me for the last time to get up and finish dinner. I didn't move, and he came charging towards me. He hit me so hard in my ear that I could hear it ringing. I screamed and screamed. I jumped up holding my ear. He then threw me across the room. He punched me in my chest and anywhere else that he could. When he missed, he hit the chair's arm rest and his knuckles bled from the impact. The mirror on the wall fell down. I blocked some of his blows coming toward my face because I didn't want anyone to know what I was going through at home.

My brother came running out of his room crying and tried to get Dad to stop hitting me. My dad, in return, hit him in the face. My brother took off running out the front door. My father took off behind him. He yelled, "Son, get back here!" I ran to the room to check on Clara. She was standing there scared. I told her to go hide under the bed and stay there until Mom came home. She told me that she wanted to go with me. Oh, I wanted to take her. I knew I couldn't take her because I was too young and I didn't know where I was going. I promised her that I was going to come back one day. I was going to make things right. I promised her that I would protect her from harm. I ran to the neighbor Ms. Jennifer's house and asked if I could use her phone to call a friend to come get me. Jennifer was at home with her three girls when they heard all the yelling and screaming coming from our apartment. We all lived on the second floor across from each other, I only knew them a few months but was able to build a close relationship with her daughters. She gave me a hug and told me to be careful and to call her if I ever needed anything. I left before my father's return. I ran down the stairs to the outside across the street to hide behind a building until my ride came.

After a couple of days of constantly searching for me, my parents found me at a friend's house. I had to leave there because I didn't want to get her family in trouble. This wasn't the first time I had run away, and I knew it wasn't going to be the last. I was fed up with everything and I wanted to be anywhere but at home with my parents. I was so mad at them that it showed on my face. My heart hardened and my demeanor was cold. My return was brief. They didn't know that I only returned to get the rest of my things and to see if my brother was okay. He had a black eye. Dad pacified his abuse to my brother by giving him an early Christmas gift. My brother was 13 at the time and he enjoyed playing with trucks, so it didn't take much to please him. Dad had given him exactly what he wanted and my brother forgave dad for the abuse. I was so disappointed but I understood that we were young and we had different opinions on life. This was something I had to do alone. My mind was already made up and there was nothing anyone could do to stop me.

Chapter 2

The Journey to a New Beginning

I pretended like I was going to work one day. I had packed a big bag. I wasn't asked about it because I always carried a lot of school books. My Mom dropped me off at work. When she drove off, I said goodbye to my friends and managers at work, and I left out of the side door. I headed to my friend's house so her mother could take me to the Greyhound bus station to catch the first bus to my grandma's house; she stayed in South Carolina. I wasn't even sure if my grandmother was going to let me come and live with her. I wasn't even sure if I was going to be in trouble when I got to her house for running away. I didn't even know if Grandma was going to send me back or not. I was scared either way. Well, it was too late to turn back, I had my ticket in hand and I was packed and sitting in my seat waiting for the bus to pull off. I was leaving for good this time vowing to never return. But my sister was still in that house, so I couldn't go far.

That bus ride was one that I will never forget. Things didn't quite go as planned. There was a snow storm. I made it all the way to Savannah, Georgia and the

Greyhound bus couldn't go any farther. The bridge that the bus had to cross over was icy. There was no other way to get to my Grandma's house. So I was stuck at the Savannah bus station for two days. I was really scared. I was by myself. There was a Burger King restaurant inside the station so I was able to eat cheeseburgers while I waited for the bridge toclear.The television stations showed up to interview people that had been stranded for days. They were asking all kinds of questions. I wanted to stay clear of the camera, so I would hide in the bathroom every time I saw the camera come into the bus station. I didn't want my parents to see me on television. I didn't want them to know where I was. I wasn't at my grandma's house yet, so I didn't want them to come get me before I made it there. Buses were leaving but they were going back to Atlanta, where I had just come from. That frustrated me. I thought that was a sign for me to go back. I ignored it and decided I would wait it out or get on another bus and maybe go somewhere else.

I had already been there two days and Atlanta was the only city they kept calling. What was I to do? Well, I wasn't going back there. So I finally decided to call my grandmother. I wanted to see if she would be mad if she knew I was on my way to her. I needed to make a decision whether or not to catch a bus somewhere else or just stay where I was. She answered the phone. I told her what happened. She didn't fuss like I thought she would. She told me that I had family nearby and that she would call so they would come and get me. I was so happy! There had been several times when a few men had offered to give me a place to stay in the hotel across the street from the bus station. Even though I said no, I thought about saying yes. I was miserable in that bus station. I wanted to relax and take a shower, eat and watch TV; anything, as long as I was out of that creepy place. Grandma told me not to move, so I didn't. I had a cousin that came up to the bus station to get me like my grandmother had asked. I didn't leave with him because I was told that my aunt was on her way to get me and take me to my grandmother's house. Grandma must have called my aunt and told her where I was. I was happy! Finally, my ride arrived. Wow, my aunt came and got me! My aunt and her guy friend drove all the way from Estill, SC in the snow for me. She wasn't fussing at all. She did tell me that my parents had been calling everywhere looking for me and that they knew I was headed to my grandmother's house and that they were coming to get me. I was saddened by the news. I had nothing to say on the ride home. It was a long and slow ride because of the snow that was on the ground. After driving for over an hour, we finally pulled up at my grandparents' house. As I walked toward the house I heard my aunt's car pull off. I entered the house and stood there for a minute not knowing what my grandmother was going to say. Waiting for her to yell at me, I held my head down for a brief moment because I felt that she would be disappointed in me, but she wasn't. She asked me if I was hungry, and I told her I was. She told me to wash up and come eat dinner. "Relax," she said. "You will be okay. You are safe now," she told me. "I'm not letting you go back. This is home now." Wow, was she for real, is that it? I wasn't in trouble or anything! She didn't even ask me what happened.

Grandma was one of the sweetest people I ever knew. I always looked forward to coming home during the summer months. She was short, with jet black hair, and she would press her hair with a straightening comb in the kitchen every Sunday morning before church. Grandma would send one of us to the store every day for a Coke and a Goody's Powder for her headache. She was a little strict, but she gave me a lot of love. We would always talk about my life in the city and she would tell me what living in the country was like. She always knew how to make me smile. She was very easy to talk to and whatever I asked for she would do her best to get it for me.

My grandfather was very laid back and very easy going. He was short with a medium built. His hair was mostly grey and thinning at the top. He had a full face of graying beard that he shaved every other day. He smile a lot and was very friendly. Even though Granddad was retired he could always be found out working somewhere with friends helping to build houses or laying bricks in somebody's yard. He started his day at 5 a.m. They live in a small country town. Before the sun came out, Granddad walked up and around town waving and saying good morning to everyone. I called him "Stormin' Norman" because rain, sleet or snow hc would do his daily walk.

It was Christmas Day. Merry Christmas, Merry Christmas! I just couldn't stop saying it. I couldn't believe it. I was where I wanted to be. I was happy. After a couple of days had gone by, Grandma and I finally talked. I told her everything. I felt that it was time that I told someone. I couldn't carry it all inside anymore. She was upset with the things I told her. My parents had told my grandma that I was doing all these bad things and that I had run off with some of their money. It was my money. I worked. I was supposed to pay a bill for my parents but I didn't. Instead I kept it and used it for a bus ticket. They were coming to get me. Grandma threatened them and told them that she would bury them both in her backyard if they came to her house. They never did. The Christmas break was finally over and it was time for me to go to school.

Grandma didn't have a car so she had someone take us to the high school so she could enroll me. I don't remember seeing Grandma ever driving a car. Registration was a difficult process. I didn't have any withdrawal papers so that was an issue. It was hard to get my school records from the school I was at in Atlanta because I left and didn't withdraw from school; therefore, they didn't have my transfer papers ready. Grandma knew the principal. He hung out with my grandfather, so they let me enroll while they worked out all the paperwork. It took some time, but they were able to contact my other school and get the paperwork they needed for me to enroll. I left Atlanta in the middle of the 11th grade. I had one year left and I would be a 1991 high school graduate. I was in a new environment and going to a new school. I was excited and a little bit nervous too. I wasn't sure if the kids at this school were going to like me or not. My cousins had come to live with us for a while as well and they also had to enroll in this new school so that made this transition a little better. Because of them, I wasn't so nervous about attending a different school and meeting new people.

As I entered the class on the first day, my stomach was in a knot. Everyone was staring at me. I walked toward the teacher and gave her my enrollment sheet. She welcomed me to her class and told my classmates my name and where I was from. I felt out of place, so I quietly walked to my seat. I didn't say much for the first couple of days. I just sat there feeling homesick, wishing I was back home at school with my friends. I had promised Grandma that if she got me into school I wouldn't leave until I finished the rest of the school term. I didn't want to break her heart, so I stayed to finish out my 11th grade year.

This new school seemed to be boring at first. It was in the country and only had a very small population of students. The school was surrounded by fields of grass, trees, and miles of highway. No buildings for miles, no stores, or fast food restaurants to run and grab a quick snack. The thought crossed my mind several times to skip class but where would I go? I would be walking for miles just to get to a gas station; besides that, the town was so small and everybody knew each other, so I knew someone would have seen me walking and would have pulled over to pick me up just to take me back to school. They would then tell my grandmother what I did. It was pointless to even think about skipping school.

There was nothing in sight that I could look at to distract my attention, so when I was bored I just stared into space and pretended that I was somewhere else. The classwork was different from the school curriculum that I had back home. The classes that I needed were not even available for me to take, so that was a problem. I only had one year left and things were not looking like I was going to get the required classes I needed at that rate. I didn't want to think about the future at that time; I was just glad that I got away and, for a minute, I felt safe.

School was kind of rough at first. I always seemed to get in trouble for not wearing dresses below the knee or shorts to a certain length. That rule didn't apply to everyone. I guess because I was new I stuck out like a sore thumb. I would always be sent home for my dress code but when others would wear or do similar things, nothing would happen to them. I had an attitude because it was so unfair that the rules only applied to certain people, and I felt because I was new and from out of town I was getting picked on a lot. This school was in the middle of nowhere surrounded by nothing but trees and grass. Once I got off the bus, I was stuck there until the end of school unless I knew someone whodrove their own car. Getting sent home was sometimes a good thing. I felt trapped being so far out in the woods. I would be excited when someone had to pick me up to take me home. After a couple of months, I was able to adjust to being at school and not get sent home as much. I didn't want my grandmother to think I was a troubled child, so I made every effort to do better whether or not the other kids had to or not.

Chapter 3

Finding My Way

My grandmother didn't work and my grandfather was retired so they didn't have much money. As soon as I could, I got a weekend job at a McDonald's on Hilton Head Island. I had just turned 16 and, this time, I could get a job without lying about my age. I had worked a few other jobs before and, due to my height, I was able to get by with people thinking I was the age I needed to be in order to work. That was a secret I kept to myself for as long as I could. I was able to get away with working under age until they would eventually ask me for a work permit that I had to get from school. Once I turned in the work permit, it told my true age and I would have to stop working. I didn't have to worry about that this time. I had everything I needed to show that I was old enough to work. There weren't that many jobs available in town. The people that lived in town would either catch buses or drive to other cities that were 45 minutes to an hour away. I had to get up at 4 am to catch a bus that took everybody to Hilton Head Island which was over an hour from my house. Getting up that early was really hard, but I had to do it. I would go back to sleep when I got on the bus. It cost seven dollars to ride the bus to work and seven dollars to ride the bus back home. With the money I made I was able to help my grandparents out the same way I helped my mom and dad. I didn't mind; I was grateful that she had allowed me to stay there. I didn't want to be a burden on her and I knew I was another mouth in the house that she had to feed, so I want it to make sure I could help make a difference while I was there. It was a struggle getting up that early to be at work at 7 a.m. and to get off at 3 p.m. and then sit and wait for two hours for the bus to come and take us back home. I didn't make much money because I could only work on weekends. I had to always make sure I saved bus fare to get back and forth to work. I always gave my grandparents most of what I earned. With what I had left, I was able to buy some of the things that I needed.

My grandparents were living off their Social Security so I knew anything I contributed would make my stay a little easier for them. I was the only girl in the house with four uncles. Yuck!!!!!! They would come home from their jobs and take their showers and mess up the bathroom. They would pee and not flush and just make a mess of the bathroom. They would never wash the tub out. I would get so mad and fuss and fuss and fuss. It didn't change anything. Every now and then Grandma would fuss at them and they would clean out the tub or pay me to do it. I was so picky about the bathroom because there was only one bathroom in the house and it would always be dirty when I wanted to take a bath. My uncles were tall like giants, except for one. They would go to work and would always come home hungry and dirty. They were always nice to me and willing to help me with anything I needed. I sometimes could earn a few dollars from them by ironing their clothes or cleaning up for them.

Back at home, my dad had been so strict about the cleanliness of the house, that I was very experienced on how things should look and smell.

Every morning at Grandma's houseI would get Pine Sol and Clorox to clean the bathroom. Grandma knew I was determined to keep the bathroom clean even though I was outnumbered by all those men. One day I mixed ammonia and Clorox in the bathroom and I poured too much. It ran us out of the house. We had to sit outside until the smell had gone away. We laughed and laughed. I knew not to do that again! Grandma and I would sometimes have a small giggle or two about it at times. I never did that again.

The time had come. Summer was almost over and another school year was approaching. I was going to the

12th grade. All I could do was think about graduation. I became sad. Sure, I had family there to support me, but what about all the friends I had back home? I had so much history in Atlanta that it wouldn't be right if I was anywhere else. I didn't feel right; I just felt out of place. I had to go back. Back to Atlanta, G-A. I knew I belonged there. I had been there all my life -since the age of three. This last year of school was so sentimental to me that if I was not back at my old school it all would have been for nothing. Most of all, I wanted to graduate with my classmates. I was going to be a senior and I wanted to feel the rush that all the other kids were feeling their last year of school. I wanted my class ring, and I wanted it from my school. So I had to go back. I talked it over with my grandmother. I wasn't sure how I was going to achieve my goal of going back to Atlanta to finish my last year of school with my old classmates, but I wanted to try. This was my last year in school and I just wanted to be where it all started. Grandma knew I was determined and she knew my mind was made up. She gave me her blessing.

I wrote my mom. I sent her the biggest Mother's Day card I could find. I told her that I loved her and that I was sorry for the way things had turned out. I was coming back home. Unfortunately, I didn't want to live with her anymore. I was going to find somewhere else to stay when I returned. I just wanted her to understand. Grandma had told me that my dad was in jail, so it was just Mom, my sister, and my brother living in an apartment in Riverdale. I wanted to run back and help. Grandma told me that I had to make a decision. Take care of them or take care of me. She told me that I was going to have to provide for myself before I could help my brother and sister. She also told me that my parents were not my responsibility and they had to get their own lives in order. I never looked at my life that way until Grandma told me that. I never hesitated when my family needed me. I would give my last and all of my time to help someone else do better. This time had to be different. I had to find my own way and let go of other people's problems and focus on graduation.

I rode the Greyhound bus back to Atlanta. This was my second time catching the bus by myself. It was a happy feeling to be going back to the city. I must admit I was a little nervous - not sure what I was going to do when I got there. Someone should have told me how to dress when traveling alone, but I didn't listen. I had on a turquoise spandex short set. All the grown men were looking at me. At that time I was just trying to be cute not realizing that I was attracting the wrong attention. The bus arrived at a station that I was unfamiliar with. I walked around a little hoping I could recognize something, anything. All I knew was thatI was downtown at the Garnett bus station and needed to be at Hapeville bus station. I went to the customer service window and the lady said that I needed $11 if I wanted to ride the Greyhound bus to the next stop, which was Hapeville - the stop I needed. I didn't have enough money. I was stranded. I was scared and I didn't know what to do. One of the guys who got off the bus that I was on came to me and offered to give me the money if I would allow him to feel my breast. I didn't know what else to do so I agreed.

He wanted me to follow him outside to the parking deck. I was nervous but I followed him. I didn't know where I was but I just wanted to get to my Mom's house. We made it to the parking deck and I stood there. The man began to touch me. I pushed away. So he tried again, asking if he could pull my pants down. That wasn't what I agreed to. He said if I wanted the money that was the only way I was going to get it. A lady saw us and yelled, "Is everything okay?!" She asked us what was going on. He walked away. I ran.

I saw him later boarding his bus. I never got the money from him. I was still feeling lost at the bus station, so I decided to walk outside. I told someone my situation and they laughed at me. They said, "Little girl, you are not far from Hapeville. You can catch the city transit and a bus and it will take you right to where you need to go for less than $2." Wow, I was happy! I had enough in my pocket to catch the train. I couldn't believe that I was that close to my destination. I ran to the train station as fast as I could. Just like I was told, I caught the train and a bus and I arrived at Hapeville Bus Station. Mom had previously told me to catch a cab from Hapeville to the house. When I arrived at my mom's house in a cab, the cab driver blew his horn and Mom came out to pay him. I never spoke about what happened at the bus station; I was just glad that lady came when she did.

I stayed with my Mom for a week, maybe two. Things were not going well for her. The lights were off. We lit candles at night for light and they had been cooking food on the barbecue grill outside every day. They had been living like this for a few weeks. Mom was doing the best she could under the circumstances. My brother was watching our little Clara everyday while Mom went to work. With me being there it kind of made things feel a little better. But within a few days of me being there, Mom lost her job. She then decided to go live with my grandmother until my dad got out of jail. My father was always in and out of jail for drinking and driving or disorderly conduct. Mom thought I was going back with them. I told her no. She couldn't believe it. "Where are you going to live?" she asked. I didn't know; I hadn't figured that out yet. She refused to leave me. She called my grandmother. Grandmother told her that she had to let me go. This was my destiny and she had to let me finish it. Grandma knew from the talk that we had that I had to finish this part of my life the way I wanted to.

We packed up the house and took all the furniture to a storage unit. Mom still tried talking to me, hoping I would change my mind. She was so scared for me. I couldn't tell her what my plan was because I didn't have one. I did promise to come home if things got too out of control. I would always call to let everyone know that I was okay. As they prepared to leave, we all began to cry. For such a short time we were a family. I just reunited with my brother and sister and I had to let them go again. I stayed behind waving goodbye as they drove off in a cab headed to the Greyhound bus station. I stayed in my mom's empty apartment for a couple of days sleeping on the floor with a blanket that mom allowed me to keep while I was thinking of where I could stay.

I remembered someone from my past who told me if I ever needed a place to stay I could always come and stay with her, Ms. Jennifer. She had three daughters that

I got along with, so I decided to go there. I didn't have her phone number so I had to walk there to ask if it was okay for me to stay with her for awhile. It took me until 1:30 p.m. to walk to her house. I stopped by the bakery in the Kroger grocery store along the way to get my favorite donut. I didn't mind the walk. It was a sunny day and I was carrying all of my belongings with me, which were a little heavy.

I made a few rest stops until I finally arrived. I knocked on the door and Ms. Jennifer answered with a surprised smile on her face. I told her my situation and, without hesitation, she gave me a place to stay. Later that evening, she told me that she wanted to introduce me to a man that could help me get back in school. The man arrived shortly after with a friend. We all talked for a few minutes, then everyone left the house leaving me alone in the house with him. He talked briefly about me going back to school and how he wanted to help me. I thanked him. But then he began to touch me and feel on my breasts. I wanted to tell him to stop, but I was scared to because I didn't want Ms. Jennifer to be mad at me and put me out for making him mad, so I didn't say anything.

He got on top of me and had sex with me. When he was finished he said he was going to take care of me and I didn't have to worry about anything. I didn't have anywhere else to go so I stayed there. I thought I was like a daughter to Ms. Jennifer, but I guess I wasn't. Ms. Jennifer lived in Riverdale across from Riverdale High School and the high school I was trying to go back to was Jonesboro High in the city of Jonesboro on the other side of town. I was going to have to figure out a plan B.

.Ms. Jennifer was a heavy beer drinker so she stayed under the influence of alcohol a lot. She always had a smile on her face. She told me that if I ever wanted to come back I could. I thanked her; I knew I couldn't come back there to stay but I would visit. Ms. Jennifer had a lot of male friends that were always coming at me and she didn't mind at all. I was seventeen, so I guess she felt that it was okay. I wasn't always comfortable with it, but sometimes I was. I was getting some attention. They were touching me in places that felt good. I wanted more of it.

But that big, fat man wouldn't go away.He was the one that Ms. Jennifer said would take care of me. He was going to help me get back in school and help pay for my graduation fees. I owed the school a lot of money for books and ROTC uniforms that I never turned in when I left to go live with my grandmother. He had a greasy

Jheri curl and smelly feet. I couldn't stand when he came around. He gave me money so I liked that part. I couldn't deal with him always wanting to get on top of me, so I had to leave there.

While staying at Ms. Jennifer's house, I met another guy that she introduced to me to. He was older than I was, but not as old as the first guy. We were together a lot at the house for about two weeks and, one day he was gone. I liked him a lot. I was sad when he left and wondered when he would ever come back. He was tall, light-skinned and had muscles. He smelled good and was so nice to me. I wanted to be with him forever but that didn't last long.

Later I ran into a friend I knew from 10th grade. We talked about me wanting to come back to Jonesboro High School to graduate. After she talked it over with her mom, she offered to let me stay with them. I left Ms. Jennifer's house as soon as I could. I wasn't mad at her, I just knew I needed a better environment. I never told Ms. Jennifer what her friend did to me because I didn't want to cause any more problems, and I suspected that maybe she already knew.

Chapter 4

There is no place Like Home

Even though I had been to Jonesboro High School before, it wasn't as easy as it was in South Carolina for me to get enrolled again. My friend's mom, Ms. Mildred, had to fill out some custody paperwork stating that she was my caretaker. Enrollment was different too. The counselor explained that due to scheduling and the class credits I took in South Carolina, I was behind in the school's curriculum and I may not be able to graduate with my class. I started to cry; that was the main reason I came back. I was so upset in the counselor's office that I started throwing things in her office. I didn't make bad grades, so I didn't understand why I couldn't graduate on time with my class. That was all I wanted to do! I had something to prove and I didn't seem to have control of anything. Things kept falling apart for me and I didn't know why or what I could do to turn things around.

What did I do so bad that God didn't want to help me? Did He see my struggle? Was He there in the house when the beatings and the cursing were being done to me? And what about when I was being shoved around and threatened with knives and a balled up fist in my face, and the voice that constantly yelled at me telling me I "wasn't going to be nothing"? Haven't I been through enough? Why so much more? Why were bad things continuing to attack me? What did I do?! I felt like I was a mistake and I wasn't supposed to be here because I had been cursed with bad luck and I didn't see things getting better for me.

The counselor said she was going to do everything in her power to find a way to help me graduate on time with my class. A couple of weeks later she called me to her office and told me that there was a program available that would allow me to graduate on time but that I would have to take a couple of classes at night. There was another high school in the area that offered these classes. The only problem was that I had to find a ride to get there. These classes were held in the evening and I worked after school so I had to find a way to work this out.

After talking to the managers at my job about what my counselor said I had to do in order to graduate, they offered to help me get back and forth to night school. I would work two hours before night class began. I would take a two-hour break to go to class and come backand clock in at work to close out the shift when I came back from class. With the help of the management team, I was able to go to night classes five days a week until the classes were complete. Every evening, one of the managers would take me to another school district where the classes were being offered -which was roughly 20 minutes away from the job - and they would be there waiting for me when I came out. The help they gave me truly blessed me and I worked even harder to graduate on time with my class.

Even though I was not living at home, I still continued to hold down a job and do the work to finish school. I had to finish school no matter what just to prove to my dad that I wasn't a dummy and a failure. I was going to be somebody and get my high school diploma if that was the last thing I did. He always used to tell me that I was going to be just like my mother. She had me when she was 13 and my brother when she was 14. Neither of my parents had their high school diploma. So he automatically assumed I was going to be the same. Well, I didn't like what he said about me and I was determined to prove him wrong. Most of all, I wanted to make sure I didn't end up with someone like him when I got married. My father used to call me so many names that I didn't think I was pretty at all. I had very low self-esteem and I didn't think I was worthy of anything! But

I figured if I was smart and got a good education, then I could get a good job and take care of myself and not have to have a man beat on me and call me names the way my dad did.

Chapter 5

Lesson Learned

While living with a close friend, I had grown close to her mom. We would sit around sometimes and talk for hours. She could warm my heart at times, and then there were times that no matter how hard I tried to fit in as part of the family, I felt out of place. Luckily, it was my senior year so I wasn't going to be there long. My plans were to graduate and join the Air Force after school.

Since my friend's mother and I were so close, she opened up and told me a few stories and I shared a few of mine - the good and the bad. She had someone special that was in the service in 1991. But we were in a war at that time -- the Gulf War -- and she worried daily about his safety. I had seen the graphic scenes on TV – people being used as human shields, a dangerous war without a real cause. She pleaded with me not to go at that time, so I didn't. Although it messed up my career plans, I decided it was best for me not to go then. But I had nowhere else to go! So I thought I might work two jobs so I could afford tuition to go back to school. Many thoughts rambled through my head about my future. It was a confusing time, but I prayed and I knew eventually I would see my way through it.

That October while in school one day I was called to the office. I pondered what it could possibly be. Upon my arrival I saw my father standing there. He had been released from jail and wanted to see me. He said he just got out that day and I was his first stop. He told me he was going to get mom and bring them back and he wanted us to be a family again. I didn't know what to say so I just smile. I gave him a hug and I started walking back to class, I wasn't happy about seeing him and I already knew I didn't want to be under the same roof with him again. A few weeks had went bye and my parents were back living in Atlanta. I was very happy for them. It saddened my parents but they knew that I had no plans of moving in with them. I enjoyed being able to see my brother and sister so I would visit every chance I could.

I was a few months away from graduation and that was all I could think about. All my hard work was about to finally pay off, I was excited knowing I was going to prove my father wrong about not graduating and making something of myself. He probably forgotten all those negative things he said to me, but I didn't. My soul was happy, one of the best feeling I had in a long time. Graduation invitation were sent out. Mom even took a few invitation her job and some of her coworkers sent cards back with money in them. I felt like a senior for the first time. Sometimes I would daydream about all the things I went through to get just to get to this very important day. I was graduating. After a few days of graduation practice, year book signing and taking pictures with friends we were ready for the actual ceremony. It's Saturday and my friend and I are at the house getting ready. Ms. Mildred drops us off a few hours early to do one last practice with our class mates. The time had come for the 1991 graduation class line up. The graduation ceremony was outside at the football stadium in Jonesboro not far from the high school. It was the first week of June and the weather was perfect. The graduation was held early that morning before the sun had a chance to come out. I was excited but somewhat nervous. I knew I pass all my classes and completed all the requirements at night school but for some reason I worried that my name was not on the list to graduate. As I sat there I looked around to see if my counselor or someone was going to pull me out of my seat at the last minute and tell me that I wasn't getting my diploma. They graduation ceremony had begun and I didn't see or hear anyone looking for me. After a few speeches and songs at was time for the class of 1991 to cross the stage. We all stood and as they called our names one by one we walked across the stage to receive our diploma. I stood there with my fingers cross. I heard my name and I took a deep breath and smile with relief. I uncrossed my finger and walked toward our principal to receive my diploma. The palm of my hands were sweaty from anxiety and anticipation. I had the evidence of success in my hand and it felt good. At the end of graduation everyone threw their hats in the air. I took my hat off and rise it up high because I didn't want to lose it or get it dirty. My parents, along with my sister and brother, came to the field to congratulate me. It was a short happy moment. As the crowd started to lingered away and there were no friends around, my dad politely ask me if he could borrow some money. Dad knew about the graduation card with money that mom had given me from her coworkers. With disappointment in my voice I told him that he could come by the house and I will give it to him. Early Sunday morning, I was woke up to Dad knocking on the door. He asked if I wanted to come to their house for Sunday dinner. "Maybe another time," I said. A few of my classmates and I were going to Six Flags and some house parties later that evening. I gave him the forty dollars and he left.

I was sitting in my room talking to Ms. Mildred one day when my boyfriend Dru came over. I had previously told her some things about him. When she saw him, she began to tell him things that I had said. She made me mad that day and I cursed at her. I was too comfortable with her. I felt so bad. It had come out so fast. I tried to take it back, and I kept saying I was sorry, but it was too late. It was over. Over a guy. A guy! He was standing there and she said something that I was embarrassed about so I cursed at her. I called her a BITCH!! What was I thinking? What came over me? We had just graduated and I was feeling excited. What had I done?

She looked at me and walked away. A few days went by before she even spoke to me. When she did, it was a sad day for me. She told me that her kids have never disrespected her the way I did and that she wasn't going to take it from me. She told me I had to leave. Well, she put me out. I was truly sad, but I had no choice but to go back to live with my parents. Wow, just that fast my life was turned upside down again. My friend was barely speaking to me, but I understood why and I didn't blame her. I was wrong for what I said to her mother. I didn't want our friendship to end the way it did, but it did. When I left her house I never saw them again. I had to quit my job because my parents didn't have a car to bring me back and forth.

I moved back in with my parents in the midst of them packing and preparing to move to another location. They had to downsize from their three bedroom townhouse in Riverdale. My parents moved into a horrible neighborhood in Forest Park, GA. We lived in a small two-bedroom apartment where I shared a room with my brother and sister. We had to clean every inch of that apartment to get it smelling and looking decent. The cleaning was disgusting but was well worth it when we finished. Mom and Dad were having some financial problems too and had to downsize until they could do better. On the inside of the house we felt like nothing had changed because of all the nice, clean furniture we had. Once we went outside into the neighborhood though, we knew we were living in the ghetto. Trash was everywhere. There was lots of graffiti all over the apartment building. As we walked around the neighborhood, we saw where people had thrown out trash, and old furniture into the streets. We didn't go outside that much because we were kind of scared of the neighborhood. I immediately started looking for jobs at nearby restaurants. I wanted to help out any way that I could and, besides, I wasn't in school anymore so I knew I had to do something. A few weeks had passed and I could tell that my father was starting to get edgy. We had settled into the apartment a little so he was getting back to his old ways. He started drinking more and more. I started having nightmare about things I had experience that I never told to anyone. One late night I was up sitting in the living room because I couldn't sleep. Mom saw me and asked what was wrong. I tried to tell her that while living with Ms. Mildred, I went to a friend's house after work one night, and her father tried to rape me. Mom looked at me with disappointment and told me to go to bed and stop looking for attention. She didn't even believe me.

Mom and Dad had gotten into a couple of arguments so I knew it was only a matter of time before he started with me. He still was a heavy drinker and he still liked to pick fights. He didn't like when he saw other men speaking to me -- he automatically assumed I was being fast. He would wait until he got drunk and tell me how he felt. I definitely wasn't going through that again, so I knew it was only a matter of time before I would be leaving there. It was about two in the morning and my father had been drinking. He woke me up and told me to come to the living room. He started yelling at me about being in our neighbor's house playing cards. I asked him what I did that was so wrong. He said I was disrespecting him and it was time for me to go. He started helping me pack my clothes and all of my belongings. He wanted me out of his house immediately. I looked over at Mom hoping she was going to say something to him, but of course, as always, Mom would blame me. She would say, "Well, you know how he is so why do you upset him?" And, "Why do you let him bother you?" She was a trip. What was I supposed to do? He was putting me out at two in the morning. He was drunk and he wasn't trying to hear anything I said. She got on my last nerve and I was starting to hate her. She made me feel like I didn't have parents, so I started to act that way. I grabbed my clothes and I left. I went to a neighbor's house to use their phone. They were up playing cards with the front door wide open so they were able to hear some of the things that were said in my parents' house. I used their phone to call a friend, but unfortunately no one was able to come get me at that time. I stood there afraid because I didn't know what to do next, nor did I have anywhere else to go. I wasn't going to ask my father to let me back in; I was done with the both of them. I went back home for a couple of months only to fall out with my father again.

There was a guy in the neighborhood named Leevay that sold drugs. He was hanging around that night, so he was able to see when I was being kicked out of the house. It was early in the morning and I was standing on my neighbor's porch with nowhere to go. Leevay walked over to me and asked if I was okay. I told him that I had nowhere to go. He told me that he had a room at the Sunburn Lodge that was around the corner from my house. I could stay there if I wanted to. I hesitated at first; I didn't know him well so I was a little nervous. He then told me that his mother was there and that I would be safe. He proceeded to tell me that he barely came to the room so he wouldn't be there to bother me. I felt a little better so I allowed him to take me to the lodge where his mother was. I was a little scared, but I didn't have a choice because I didn't have anywhere else to go. It was a quiet, slow walk for me; I had a lot on my mind. I couldn't believe I had allowed myself to be put in this situation again with my mom and dad. I hadn't even been living with them for a full month, and I trusted them like I was at home again and everything was going to be okay. Even though I was walking at a slow pace, we arrived very quickly. He opened the door. Slowly, I entered the room. All the lights were off. Leevay's mom was sleeping. I tried to be as quiet as possible because I didn't want to wake her. He helped me put my things away and told me that I would be okay, and then he left.The room was small but it had two beds in it, a refrigerator, stove, and a bathroom. I stared into space for a minute until I finally fell asleep. I laid cross the bed wondering what his mom was going to say to me when she woke up. Well, she never did for a couple days. I was there for almost three days before I finally met her. She worked a lot, so when she was not working, she was sleeping. For three days I was in the room with his mom who didn't know who I was or anything about me. The day finally came when she woke up to meet me. She said, "Hi," and asked, "Who are you?" I told her my name and told her what happened and that her son Leevay told me it was okay for me to stay here. Her name was Sherrita. She smiled and said, "My son will help anybody in need." She asked me if I was okay and if I needed anything. I said, "Nothing right now." I told her I was scared and I felt alone. She told me to relax and that I could stay there as long as I needed to. I was thankful. I just needed some time to think and figure out my next move.

I had applied at the McDonald's around the corner from where I was staying when I was with my parents. Ms. Sherrita worked there too, so she helped me get the job. She was also working at the truck stop not far from McDonald's, so she could walk to work. I liked how Ms. Sherrita was working two jobs and I wanted to do the same. Two weeks later I started working at Zesto across from the McDonald's. I didn't have anywhere else to go and nothing else to do. I decided to work so I wouldn't just sit around thinking about all the bad things that were happening to me.

One day there was a knock at the door and it was my dad. I looked through the peephole and saw him. I froze. I felt angry and frustrated all over again. I had nothing to say to him so I sat back down on the bed. I asked Ms. Sherrita to answer the door and to tell him that I wasn't there. She went to the door, as soon as she opened it, I could smell his alcoholic breath, and I could tell by the tone of his voice that he had been drinking. I definitely didn't feel like being bothered with that. Ms. Sherrita told him that I wasn't there. He told her he was my father and he was worried about me and wanted to make sure that I was okay. Leevay had told him that I was staying at the Lodge with his mom. I didn't understand why he waited until he was drinking to check on me. Oh now you want to talk to me! It seemed like the only time he wanted to deal with things was when he was drinking. I had nothing to say to him and I didn't want to see him for a long time.

I continued to work two jobs for a while. We lived in that Lodge for a few more months until we found an apartment. We agreed to move in with some of Sherrita's friends that also needed a place to stay, but that only lasted a few weeks. It was a two-bedroom apartment that was very crowded with all of us staying there. Eventually, Ms. Sherrita and I were able to get our own apartment in the same neighborhood just one building over. We officially became roommates. We agreed to split the bills in half. I had my own room and I didn't have to answer to anybody. We were living in some apartment that were next to the apartments were my parents were staying, I could walk through a path and be at my parents house in five minutes. I worked two jobs so I was able to pay my way. I was happy but felt different - even a little strange - having an older woman as my roommate. I got used to it. It was my first time having my own place but, with Sherrita guiding me, I felt okay. Even though my parents' apartment was across the walkway I never went to visit.

I knew I wasn't at home anymore and I had to trust somebody else with my life. I didn't know how I was going to do that, so I just worked a lot - blocking out all bad memories and the scary thoughts I had. I prayed a lot, hoping that God was listening and maybe one day He would tell me what to do.

I vowed never to go back home to my parents and I meant it. I was so hurt, angry and disappointed, which, in turn, made me more determined to stay away. I didn't want to ever have to ask them for anything. My heart became so bitter towards them that I would say that my parents were dead, or sometimes I would just say that I hadn't spoken to them in years. I was on my own and that was all I knew. I felt likeI had no one to turn to or call when I needed advice or help. So I couldn't look back, I couldn't quit, and most of all I couldn't fail. If anything ever happened to me, where was I going to go? What was I going to do, and who was going to care? I had only me. I had to learn how to manage my life day by day, step by step. It wasn't easy, but I was determined. I think it was my anger that drove me for a while. It gave me energy to push forward, even when I didn't see a way through my struggles. I wanted to be something more than what I was. I wasn't sure how I was going to do it but I just wanted to.

Chapter 6

Living past the pain

I started having lots of nightmares. They were always about a man standing in the woods. I could never see his face, only his shadow. I knew it was my real father. I would wake up crying. I only met him one time and I don't remember his face. In my dreams, I struggle to see his image trying to look into his eyes. I always wondered why he didn't come around or visit me, or why he just left me. I had been abused and mistreated by my stepfather, and my real father never knew it. Mom never talked about him much, so I didn't have a clue of where to begin searching for him. I had a lot of unanswered questions that I knew I had to seek answers to so that my dreams would go away. For now I had to bury those thoughts and ideas because I was dealing with so many other things that couldn't wait.

I remembered I made a promise to my little sister that I wanted to keep. I promised her that I would always be there for her and I wasn't going to let her down.

Every Christmas, I would always make sure that Clara was okay and that she received presents from Santa

Claus. She found out quickly that I was her Santa Claus. During those times Dad couldn't hold down a job and his drinking and drug habits were getting worse.

My parents moved around a lot. Mom had to hold the family down during the times my father went back and forth to jail. Those times were hard for everybody. There were times when they lived without lights until Mom could get up enough money to cut the lights back on. I would help out when I could. I must admit there were times that past memories would make it hard for me to come around, sometimes for months. Even though I was struggling in my heart with things that my parents had done to me, I wouldn't stay away too long because my sister and brother were there and I didn't want them to think I had abandoned them.

It didn't take long before my brother finally left. I guess he couldn't take the fighting with dad anymore either. Thadd was getting older and had been working out to build up his body muscle. He was short and very petite and he didn't like that. He worked constantly to get strong and gain more body weight so Dad wouldn't be able to throw him around the way he used to. He was very small most of his life. Through his anger his he worked hard to become more solid in weight.Lifting weights helped him feel like more of a man and he felt he could use his strength to defend himself when needed. I was kind of disappointed that he left because I felt that he wasn't ready, but who was I to decide when someone was ready to leave that type of lifestyle? He had to be about sixteen and in the 10th grade when he left. I was worried because he was still in high school. I remember how hard it was for me to finish school and I didn't think he had that same self-discipline. His determination was very different from mine.School was not as important for him as it was for me. He chose to get out in the streets to make a living for himself by working odd jobs and selling drugs. I am not sure where he stayed at times. He was working and hustling, so he was able to provide for himself by living in hotels or with friends. He saved up some money and bought a car, but he didn't keep that very long. He was hardheaded and full of anger, which cause him to make a lot of bad decision. I found out later in life that he was not only selling drugs that he also started using drugs. He said he did the drugs to stay awake at night while he was out trying to make his money. I didn't agree, but I didn't care what he did as long as he was okay. The anger my brother carried inside made it hard for him to focus on school or even keep a steady job. I knew if he didn't get some help and change his attitude that one day he was going to end up in jail. He was his own boss and he wasn't listening to anyone.

I was very uncomfortable that Clara was at home by herself. When my brother was there I didn't have to worry so much about her. Our parents were very strict at times, and having another sibling around helped the days go by easier. I worried about how Clara was going to be without having my brother or me there to keep her company.

I am not saying that every day was a nightmare. There were some good times too.There were times when dad would take us to the movies or barbecue at the house and hangout with us joking and laughing. We went on long walks and he would always try to say things to encourage us to finish school and do better than he did. He would always tell us that he loved us. We knew he did, but just didn't like how he showed it. Some day's Dad could drink his beer and liquor and want to play and sing with us all night. Dad and I would stay up until the sun came up talking about anything that came to mind: All the people from his family that had passed away and the family that he had in New Jersey that he barely knew. I would always ask when we were going to visit them and he said he wouldn't know where to begin. He left when he was a kid and doubted if he would remember anybody. Then there were the times when he would get so drunk that he didn't know who I was.

I remembered after high school that I wanted to join the military, but I didn't know how I was going to leave for the Air Force and at the same time protect my sister who was only six years old. I was very conflicted about what to do with my life because my Dad had not changed, and I knew it would only be a matter of time before he did things to her they way he did me. I wanted to be right there when he did. I was going to protect her and be there for her for whenever the day came that she wanted out. Mom, at the time, was just impossible to talk to. I could tell that the burden of abuse in their marriage weighed heavily on her. She always thought that things would get better. She always overlooked the things that he did and blamed his ways on his drinking. She was not listening and she definitely didn't want to see what was really going on. I don't know why she stayed, but she did. I couldn't control my Mom's destiny, but I was going to try to make sure my sister had one.

I didn't join the Air Force because Clara was going to be by herself and I didn't want her to ever feel that way. I took enough beatings and name-calling for the both of us and it made me sick mentally. I wanted to make sure she had a better chance at life than I did. I wanted her to enjoy growing into her teenage years and entering into adulthood. Most of all, I wanted to be there when Dad would get drunk and mistakenly go into her room. I will never forget that day; we had only been in school for a few weeks after returning from our summer break. I had just come home from school, wearing my ROTC uniform. It was a Tuesday. As usual, Dad had been drinking and Mom was working the night shift. I was preparing supper and doing laundry. Dad was talking to me while I prepared dinner. He was saying things that I really didn't understand. He was slurring his words and it just sounded like a bunch of mush. I laughed with him and pretended like I understood every word he said. Mom said laughing with him would keep him calm, so I tried it. While trying to fix a sandwich, he dropped a piece of bread on the floor. I gave a soft giggle; that made him mad. He looked at me with anger in his eyes and grabbed me by my neck. I had a knife in my hand, he took it. He laid me on the floor. He told me he would cut me with the knife for laughing at him. He then picked the bread up off the floor and pushed it into my mouth. He finally let me up, and resumed talking to me like nothing had happened. I was scared to death and I began to cry. I tried not to let him see me crying, so I turned back to the sink area where I was preparing food. He started going back and forth with my name. One minute I was Marilyn and the next he was calling me my mother's name. I told him that I was not her, but he continued saying it anyway. He grabbed me, looked me in my face and told me that he loved me. He then kissed me in the mouth. Dad has kissed me in the past when we said good night, so I thought it was okay until he wouldn't let me go. I tried to pull away, but he was stronger than me, so it was hard to get away. I wasn't trying to accuse him of anything; I was just uncomfortable with it. I went to my room to fold the laundry. I needed to breathe and to get away from him, but there he came, staggering up the stairs. He entered my room - talking to me as if I was my mom again. He sat down beside me on the bed and he tried to kiss me again while forcing himself on top of me. It instantly freaked me out, so I pushed him off of me and took off running out of the house. I went up the street to a friend's house. I didn't want to go back home ever again. I was scared and I didn't want to see him again. It had been raining, so it was hard to notice that I had been crying. I didn't say much when I first got there. I tried to hold in the tears for as long as I could. It was dinnertime and they wanted me to eat with them. I tried to say that I wasn't hungry, but they insisted. While sitting at the dinner table tears began to flow from my eyes and they instantly knew something was wrong. My friend took me to her room where we could talk and I told her what happened. Her mom agreed to let me stay the night as long as my mom knew where I was. So I called my mom and told her what happened. She seemed to be very upset and told me everything was going to be okay. I told her that I didn't want to ever go back home and she said she understood. I went to school the next day wearing some of my friend's clothes. I went to school like nothing had happened. I was kind of happy that I didn't have to go back home for a while. I just knew that Mom was going to let me go and stay with my grandmother. I was so happy to be getting out of that house. It was around lunch time when my mom came to the school to check me out. I wasn't expecting her. She said that we needed to talk. She told me that I had to come back home. She said I could leave home when I turned 18 and had graduated from high school. She said, "Your father was drunk," and she said that he didn't remember anything. Mom then tried to tell me her story about when she was a little girl; she went through some similar things with her siblings' fathers. She hoped that I would understand. She was trying to let me know that I wasn't the only person to ever experience something like this. But that was also one of the reasons she left home at an early age to live with my stepfather; she was tired of being touched by men that came to the house. Was this supposed to make me feel better? I felt betrayed. What was she trying to say: That I should be okay with what just happened to me? Did she even care about how I was feeling? I was scared and she didn't even try to comfort me. She wanted me to act like it didn't happen and to intentionally brush it aside. She wanted me to look at it as one of life's bad experiences, or a little mishap on my dad's part. Well, it may have been a "mishap" or just "part of life's bad experiences" to her, but I was a little girl hurting on the inside and Ijust wanted to die. When we arrived at the house, I was so scared that I ran to my room and locked the door. I felt all alone. It felt as though I was being punished by God.When I looked at other families, their moms and dads were not fighting or mistreating them the way my parents treated us. I didn't understand why God didn't send help for us or take us out of that terrible situation. I later learned that God was not punishing me and that He had been there the whole time. I knew that until Clara was out of harm's way I couldn't go far. I just wasn't ready to take the chance of her feeling like she had no one to turn to in her time of need. It was important for me to be the voice she needed to help her survive anything that harmed her.

Chapter 7

A Sister's Love

Those past experiences gave me nightmares and maybe a few mental issues and I didn't want Clara's mind to travel down that same path. She was young and still had a chance to have her mind free and to be able to sleep in peace at night. I wanted her to like who she saw when she looked in the mirror. I wanted her to play sports and to go on dates with her friends without having to be bothered with the problems that existed at home. I wasn't living at home, but I would always visit her and talk to her to make sure she was okay. I would leave money underneath the outside door mats so she could eat lunch and have money to go on school field trips. When she would cry about things, I would always tell her to remember she had me and she had no reason to cry.

Whatever she needed I was going to make sure she had it. She didn't think that she was pretty, so I would always make her look in the mirror and explain to me what she didn't like about herself. I remember taking her to the hair salon with me to get her hair done and she had the biggest smile on her face that I ever saw. Oh my God she was smiling! "Where did that come from?"

I asked. I look pretty she said. I really like my hair. She said I always knew how to make her feel happy even when sadness was around. I would always go pick her up to get her out of the house and to keep her mind free from all that bull crap that my dad would say to her. He was still acting the same. Every weekend he would get drunk and argue with her about anything he could. She would always call me crying, and I would come pick her up and keep her until Mom came home. I never encouraged her to run away like I did. I would always tell her that I was there whenever she needed me.

In the meantime, I wanted to show her Atlanta. On my off days we would get on the MARTA bus, go downtown, and then catch the bus to Lenox Mall. We would visit all the stores and eat Cinnabons. Those were our favorites. Every time we got together we had to go to the mall a get a Cinnabon first. That was our sisterly tradition.

I tried to get Clara out as much as I could - especially during the summertime. When school was in she would come over on the weekends. I shared an apartment in College Park with my uncle Gerald. We had been roommates for several years. Gerald moved from my grandmother's house to work and live in Atlanta. My parents were okay with that and those visits gave us time to hangout and have fun with each other. Most weekends I had to work. I would go to work, but later I would call Clara and she would catch a cab to my job after all the head managers had left for the evening.

Clara was too young to work, so I would sneak her to my job at night to help wash dishes and make biscuits. Her eyes would stretch wide at the shock of receiving money for the work she had done. She would smile with a confused look on her face, as if she was thinking, "Why is my sister paying me for helping her?" Before she could get the question out of her mouth, I would reply that she had earned it and it was hers to spend on whatever she wanted.

Every chance she got to come over to my house I would always find ways to allow her to come to work with me in order to earn some pocket money. Clara was very shy and fragile and I was trying to help her loosen up and enjoy her life. She was coming of age; she liked boys but she thought that she wasn't pretty enough and that no one would talk to her. And what would she say if they did? So with the money that she earned while working with me, we would go to the malls and pick out things that made her feel pretty. She would always buy the same things: T-shirts and jeans. I would take her to the beauty parlor with me and let them do her hair and go to the nail shop to get our toes and nails done. I would constantly tell her that she was pretty and that she just had to glamorize herself with some accessories.

We would stand in the mirror for hours dancing in our underwear, pretending that we were beauty queens. I wanted her to know that she was beautiful inside and out, and that she must believe that no matter what anybody else thought. I would laugh and say, "Just wait, you are going to get your share of boyfriends." "You are so pretty," I would say, "and lots of boys are going to ask you to go out with them. Some of them will be good and some of them will break your heart." She didn't quite understand what I was saying, but I knew she would one day.

When Clara turned 15, I gave her a job at the restaurant where I worked. There was a SunTrust Bank right across the street and I helped her start an account there. When she received her weekly check, she would put some in the bank and help Mom out around the house with buying things for the house. I didn't want them to take her money, but I wanted Clara to understand that Mom and Dad would allow her to continue working with me if she helped out around the house.

I had started working when I was 14; I'd lied about my age so that I could get a job to help my mom out with the bills. I gave up wanting to play basketball because I felt that I needed to help my family. I figured if I could help around the house, maybe then things at home would be the way they should be. Our water and lights were always getting cut off. The rent people were always knocking on the door. I wanted to help out. I thought if I got a job that they wouldn't argue so much and maybe all the mean things that were happening to us would stop.Boy, was I wrong!I continued to work just to get out of the house anyway. I learned quickly that keeping a job was going to be my ticket out. I had no one to run to or to tell all my problems to, so I had to depend on myself for everything.

Clara was going to be different; she had me. I vowed to myself that I would always be there for my little sister. There were times when I had to survive on my own and it was scary. I met a lot of mean people along the way. Every week that Clara got paid, I told her to give Mom money because she needed help with the bills and it was a sign of respect. This way, they would know that she was being helpful around the house. Most importantly, I wanted her to save some of her money and to see how much she could save for school. In doing so, she could buy all the latest fashions that all her friends were wearing. She was getting of age; she was very full-figured, and I knew the things that she really needed were too expensive for my parents.

Money at home with mom and dad was as tight as always. I wanted her to take her money and learn how to shop for herself. Besides, it made things a little easier for my parents to focus on paying their bills.

I personally took it as an opportunity for her to get the things that I couldn't get in life -I so wanted her life to be better than mine. She made a lot of money that year working with me. She complained a lot about the long hours and having to stay at work until I finished my work -causing us to sometimes be there all night. So when she turned 16, she decided to get a job close to her house, and I agreed. She was still living at home with Mom so I really didn't have any say-so in the matter. She knew I was a call away whenever she needed me.

I was having a baby. Henry and I had been together for several years now and even though we talked about kids we never official agreed to when would be a good time. I was scared because of all the painful childbirth stories I heard and I didn't know if I would be a good mother. Pregnancy was hard for me. I was sick all the time and some days I couldn't even get out of bed. We lived in a townhouse apartment and I could smell scents coming from the kitchen downstairs. I tried eating fruit, Jell-O, cereal and noodles. Nothing worked. After eating, within a few minutes I would be bent over a trash can, throwing up everything I ate. The pressure from my stomach trying to push up any residue that was left inside me from the food I tried to digest would push on my bladder and I would instantly start discharging urine in all of my clothes. I didn't leave the house much but whenever I did, I always kept a change of clothes with me. I was a son and he didn't want anything nor did he like perfumes or any type of scent lotions. Dad tried to convince Clara that I wasn't going to have time for her anymore but I made sure she knew that she had nothing to worry about. Months of sickness had finally come to an end. I started having slight stomach cramps but wasn't concerned with them. I spoke to Henry while he was on his lunch break and he ask if I needed him to come on and I said no. I had been on the phone all day talking to some friends and resting when I could. Henry called again that evening to see if I needed him to come home or should he go to his second job. I said I was fine. Henry notice that my voice had change and I was taking deeper breathe then I did earlier when he called. Henry was working two jobs because he was paying off some bills and wanted save money to buy him a new car. Since this was the first time I ever felt any type of pain I assume that it would eventually go away if I just stayed relaxed. Within minutes, Henry was coming through the front door running up the stairs to see how I was doing. I was having contractions, still trying to talk on the phone. My friend Vickie had gotten arrested for a traffic violation and needed someone to bond her out of jail. I was trying to make calls for her and see if someone could go get her or I was going to go to her rescue as soon as the cramping stopped. Henry took the phone from me and said goodbye and hung up. With a sad look on my face I asked why he did that. He looked at me, smiled, and said, "You are having contractions and you need to worry about yourself for now." I really wanted to make sure my friend was okay but the contractions had grown stronger and Henry wasn't letting me get back on the phone. After calling my doctor to give them an update we decided that we should walk around the neighborhood. Holding hands and stopping a few times when contractions felt too strong to move, we were able to walk a few times around our apartment complex. Contractions started coming a lot more often and stronger so we called the doctor again. They suggested that we go to the hospital. I called my parents so they could meet us there. I was so nervous. I wasn't ready to deliver. I hoped that it was false alarm and that I have a few more weeks to prepare. I could tell Henry was nervous because of the way he was driving. I felt every speed bump, sharp swirly turn and blowing his horn and every car that was driving slowly in front of him. We arrive to Southern Regional safely and my parents and Clara was there waiting on us. I was place in a wheel chair and within minutes I was admitted to labor and delivery. Midwife came from my doctor's office and check on me. She suggested that I try to walk around the halls a few times to help the progress. Mom, Clara and I walked the halls while Dad and Henry sat in the waiting room. We walked for almost two hours and then I told them I wanted to rest. The nurse helped me get into a bed and hooked up monitors on my stomach and an IV into my arms for fluids. Since I wasn't going to walk anymore, the midwife decided that she would break my water to prepare me for labor. I started to tremble from fear of not knowing what was going to happen next. The midwife told my mom that she was going to go make some coffee and because this was my first child this could take some time. Within a few minutes I started having stronger contractions and they were coming faster. I didn't have time to breathe before the next contraction came. I was frustrated and wanted to go home. I tried to get up but of course mom called for the nurse and she tried to stop me. Henry came into the room to see what he could do to calm me down. I was in so much pain that I was yelling and screaming at him. I tried to bite my mom and I wanted to fight Henry. I yelled at him until he promised not to get me pregnant ever again. The midwife came rushing back to the room and with surprise in her eyes she saw that I had dilated all the way and she could see my son's head crowning. After a few calming words, she convinced me to relax and I allowed her to help me have our baby. I wanted an epidural but she said it was too late for that. She couldn't give me anything because I was minutes away from seeing my son. The midwife said to me, "If you give me five minutes this will all be over." I was ready for it to be over with, so I agreed. The room was hot and I was pouring sweat. The nurse didn't have time to prep me so my mom had to hold one leg and Clara held the other. Henry was holding my hand, allowing me to squeeze it as much as I needed to. The midwife changed quickly out of her leather black skirt, white muscle shirt and her knee-high riding boots. The nursing staff helped her put on her scrubs and white jacket and we were ready. She told me to push, and I did, but not much due to fear of more pain and my body being ripped apart. A contraction was approaching and I was to push as hard as I could. Pushing and yelling as loud as I could, he arrived. Henry looked down to make sure our son had ten fingers and ten toes. Macarion Monte' Gentry was born 6 lbs and 8oz. Henry went to the waiting room to tell my father the good news. Clara was excited that she was allowed to cut the umbilical cord. I was later taken to another room where I would stay and rest for the next two days. After a few visits with me and the baby, Dad and Mom left but allowed Clara to stay with me to help me out through the night. I was so happy she was there with me. Henry had to work the next day so he went home as well. I was very weak and Clara assisted me with going to the restroom, breastfeeding, and Macarion's diaper changes. She could only stay the first night because she had to go to school the next day.

A few months went by and Clara started running away from home. My dad had started back on his drunk spells, and he was picking on her. She reacted by running away. She would always find a phone to tell me where she was going and that she was okay. I would let my parents search for her for a day or two before I would tell them where she was. I waited and waited for her to tell me to take her away and never bring her back. She never did. I told her she was not alone. No matter what she did or where she went, she had promised to always call me. I didn't want to tell her to leave because that was what I wanted; I wanted it to be when she got ready. She would just look at me and say, "Okay."

My brother had already left home a couple of years before that, so Clara was at home by herself. I had no choice but to stay close. Clara would always leave home when things got too out of hand for her to handle. The tears in her eyes reminded me of what I was going through during those tough times in my life. I began to feel the hatred in my heart. The nightmare had come back. I wanted to tell my parents how I was feeling. I wanted to explain it, but I couldn't. Mom was still trying to patch up things at the house and she wasn't trying to listen to anything that was negative - especially from me. I was living on my own and to try to explain how I was affected by my past was unreal. I knew as long as my sister was going through her mental and physical abuse that I would go through it too, again and again. I couldn't erase it. I wanted my past to be just that. Would it ever stop? Would the nightmares ever go away? Then that day finally came. . . I will never forget that final call.

Dad had been drinking. He was arguing with my sister. Of course Mom was at work. Mom did the best she could when she was around to help out with making dad sit down somewhere and leave Clara alone. Mom would spend most of her time crying her eyes out, asking why he couldn't just drink his liquor and not bother anyone. Clara would manage to call me to tell me what was going on and when I arrived. He would see my car pull up and act like nothing was wrong. It was too late for that! I had the look of death in my eyes and I was coming to destroy anything in my way. This was not the first time Clara had to call me to get her out of the house or to calm my father down. I had to leave my job several times when she called to challenge my father's behavior towards Clara. My father's drinking seem to me getting more intense. The Constant name calling and bullying Clara Space was to overwhelming for the both of us so I told Clara to pack her bags and that she would not ever coming back. I was scared shitless to make a stand against my parents and I didn't want them to hate me. I knew in my heart that I was doing the right thing and I had prayed to God for strength because I didn't know the challenge I would face. All I had was faith and my painful memories, and I was ready to stand on those alone. I didn't want my mom to hate me. I hoped she would understand that it was for the best. As the older sister, I felt obligated to Clara to pull her out of her unhealthy environment and to save her beauty within. I hoped she would have better childhood memories than me. She needed me to tell her that it was time for her to leave because she was that same scared little girl that I had been, and she needed a push to leave. I fought my way out and I was determined to be there to help her get out; hopefully without the fighting.

I was at ease knowing that I had stood up for her, she would be safe, and I wouldn't have to worry anymore about what was going on with her in that house. With her being with me, I hoped it would also help me let go of some of the hatred, pain, and anger that I had in me that I had been dealing with for some time now. You would think that since I was grown and on my own I would have forgotten all the things that I had experienced when I was living at home. Unfortunately, that wasn't the case because I still felt lots of pain and sorrow.

I had to pay close attention to my attitude in order to make sure that it didn't get the best of me, so I tried to stay focused and busy. I don't smoke or drink so I didn't have a temporary escape or anything that could relax me from my thoughts. I didn't want to hide behind drugs or alcohol like my father did to deal with his life experiences. I think that the fact that he never dealt with his abusive childhood and the death of his mom is why he didn't know how to express himself other than being mean and violent toward us. My dad's mom died when he was 13. He had been mad at her and God since then. She promised him that she was going to get better after her last surgery. Well it was her last; she died from cancer. Looking at his life and the way we were treated, I had to find a way to be different and hope for a better life for all of us. Me being the oldest, I figured it was my job to protect my brother and sister in any way I could, if they were willing to let me. I felt as though I was chosen to break the generational curse. I had to succeed at everything so that my sister and brother would follow.

If I showed them a better way, then maybe I could motivate them to push hard in doing the same thing. As time went on, I realized that Clara still had a lot of stored-away pain and bad memories of her own. My brother Thadd was also still struggling with a lot of bottled up anger inside him caused by the abuse that he experienced living at home with our parents. He acted as if he was pretty much angry at the world. He had little patience with people and it seemed as though he couldn't keep a job anywhere. The two of us weren't getting along either. My brother started having kids. His bad attitude and the fighting seemed to be a part of him. The mothers of his children were having a hard time trying to deal with him. I didn't understand at that time what was causing all his crazy mood swings. We argued so much and I was not sure of anything. I was too young to see what he was so mad and angry about. I just kept him at a distance and tried not to deal with him unless it was necessary.

Chapter 8

A Mother's Broken Heart

Henry and I grew apart and decide that it was best for the both of us to separate. Due to the apartment complex being bought out by the airport, I was able to relocate to another apartment subdivision with no expenses out of my pocket. I didn't waste much time making sure that Clara felt safe. I got her into a school in my district so that she could actually be happy and have friends like she always wanted; and she could even invite them over to the house. I could hear them laughing and gossiping about their own teenage problems. I didn't realize it until later that she had picked up some bad habits in order to handle the stress in her life. Little did I know that she was still unhappy. She was torn on the inside and only time and lots of prayer was going to fix that. She smoked cigarettes. Of all things to do she was a smoker. Yeah, I know it could have been worse, but I hated cigarette smoke. She didn't even tell me that she had picked up smoking, but I figured it out eventually. I would see cigarette boxes in her clothing drawer and when I questioned her about them she would say that she sold them to her friends at work. When her clothes smelled like cigarettes, she would say that she had been around people that had been smoking. She always had an excuse for every question I had. Finally, after talking to my mom on the phone, it came out. Mom told me that Clara had been smoking for a couple of months and she was okay with it. Mom figured it was just a phase that Clara was experiencing and that maybe one day she would grow out of it. Wow, I was tripping! A phase! Is it that simple? She can have a smoking phase? She was too young to be smoking. She was still in high school. I just didn't understand. I was shocked that my parents knew and were okay with it. I didn't understand that at all. Maybe because she was not at home anymore and Mom just didn't care. Or was it her guilty conscience that made her not care what Clara did, and was she just glad that Clara was stopping by to visit on occasion?

Mom realized that everything that had happened at home had caused her to lose her children. We all left home before the age of 18. Mom was very disappointed about that. As I look back, those were some hard times - not only for us, but also for my mom. She wasn't perfect, but I know she loved us and if she could have had her way, we would all still be at home. She couldn't do anything to change the rough discipline we received, my dad's alcoholic drinking, or his drug problems - along with his outrageous mood swings and his violent behavior. Mom was just stuck in a world that she didn't know how to handle. She felt obligated as a wife to be there for my father because she knew he had nobody else.

She wanted her children's love and she also wanted her marriage. Through the good, the bad, and the ugly, we knew that Mom was never going to leave our dad. That was something that we would never understand; we just hoped and prayed that she would find the happiness that she deserved one day before God call her home. I never understood my family. I was slightly embarrassed with the fact that this was the family I had. I wanted normal parents like everyone else had. I wanted to have children one day and wanted it to be okay for them to spend the night at their grandparent's house. I wanted normal conversations and cookouts where we could all sit around, laugh and have a good time.

I was so busy worrying about dad's drinking habits and his violent temper that I didn't want to be around him, and I knew I wasn't going to let any child of mine stay in that house. I love my parents, but there was a part of me that was still hurting and I knew that I hadn't yet forgiven them. I was bitter and still mad at my parents - especially my father because he never changed. It was like he was getting worse the older I got. Thadd, Clara and I were not living at home anymore to prevent some of the things he did. Dad would get drunk while Mom was at work and burn up the food because he would be passed out on the floor. She would come home thanking God that the house hadn't burned down. Mom started to grow weary and get depressed. She never knew what to expect when she came home from work. Some days she would come home and he would lock her out the house for hours just because he felt like it. As usual, he had been drinking and was just being mean to her. Whenever this happened, she would just sit in the car or on the porch until he cooled off and decided that she could come back into the house. A few hours would go by before he would let her back in. She was the only one working most of the time. Bills were piling up and she didn't know how she was going to get caught up. She worked really hard to keep a roof over their heads and even begged us at times to move back in to help them out. Of course we said no. Mom had always been a strong person, but as time passed, I saw that she was growing weary. She looked stressed and very tired. Mom started drinking beer a lot to cope with the things she was dealing with. But she didn't complain at all. She would always smile and say that everything would be okay. As she wiped tears away that bore her frustration, I knew she didn't truly believe that, but she was hoping for a miracle. My dad's abusive drinking had finally taken a toll on her. Some days it was hard for Mom to even get out of bed. She would drink beer until it made her sick. My dad would call me complaining that my mom had a hangover and their house was dirty. I tried to explain to him that he was the cause of it, but of course he didn't listen. There was no way to convince my mom that they needed to separate in order for the both of them to get some help. My parents had been together since high school and separating was not an option for her. Sometimes I felt as though she was prepared to die as long as he was okay. Mom had gotten so depressed that one time we had to check her in to a mental hospital for treatment. She stayed there a few days only to come out and face the same problems she had when she went in: My father.

My dad drank so much that he truly never paid attention to the people and things around him that he was hurting. He had his own life struggles to deal with. There would be times when he would get on the phone and call anybody that would listen to him cry about his mom, his life, and anything else he could mention before they hung up the phone. He was hoping for some sympathy from someone. I guess you can say he never knew how to 76 deal with his past trials and tribulations, and new issues just grew on top of the old ones. We could never figure out what he wanted people to do for him. Half of the time, we didn't even know what to say to my father. There were times he would call me crying, saying he was sorry if he ever mistreated us. He would try to explain his childhood problems and that no one taught him how to love. He missed his mother dearly and never got the chance to say goodbye before she died from cancer. He felt abandoned because she was all he had. He would always say that he didn't have much of a father figure, so he didn't know how a father should act. That was his excuse for being so mean. He felt as though people had mistreated him all his life and this was the only behavior he knew. We all have our own pains from bad memories, rejection or some type of abuse. They can be worked out through prayer, counseling and family support, but a person has to be willing to get that needed help. So why couldn't he?

Chapter 9

Harm's Way

Some time had passed. Clara was older and was making her own decisions - some good and some bad. She didn't care much about school anymore and she stopped going in the middle of her12th grade year. She wasn't looking back on that. I wasn't too happy about that but I hoped, in time, that she would go back and finish. This was something that our parents didn't get the opportunity to achieve, so it was important to me that we did. I guess you could say that I was a bit strict. I constantly stayed on my sister - fussing about everything she wasn't doing right or up to my standards. I just wanted the best for her and I think she just wanted to be a teenager. She didn't look at life the way I did and no matter how hard I tried to make her see life through my eyes, she didn't. She was going to do things her way whether I liked it or not. She hung out with friends drinking and smoking. She worked a little, but for a while she didn't. The day had come for us to go our separate ways. I had to move out of the apartment we were living in because of all the loitering Clara and her friends had been doing while I was at work. I was so mad at her. So she decided to move in with some friends that she was hanging out with in the apartments. They were a young couple, around Clara's age, that stayed in the building behind where we lived. They smoked, drank, and played cards together all the time. They allowed Clara to sleep on their couch and she was okay with it. She had no rules to follow and could make her own decisions without someone like me constantly looking over her shoulders. She had met a guy that had been hanging out over there, so that gave her another reason to stay. Her guy friend gave her money to help her with things she needed while staying with her friends. I was so disappointed. I didn't understand why she wanted to live like that, why she didn't have a job, and why she was so comfortable with not having her own money. I asked about this guy she was dating and she told me that he was living with his girlfriend. I was speechless. Clara said that she didn't care because he was always spending time with her and giving her money. She wasn't living with me so I couldn't say anything.

One day I let Clara use my car and she came to pick me up from work with this guy sitting on the passenger side of the car. She got out to let me drive, went to the passenger side of the car, and her guy friend moved to the back seat. When I got into my car it smelled of alcohol. This guy was so drunk that my car smelled like alcohol was poured directly on the floor. I looked at her hard. The guy began to try to have conversation with me. He was sitting behind me, touching on my shoulder, and patting my arms. I repeatedly asked him to stop. Clara had to ask him several times to stop, but he was so drunk and he was not paying any attention to us. We were headed to drop them back off to where she was staying. The guy was still being rude to me, so I pulled over and put him out on the street, a block away from where she stayed. I pulled off in the car with her and I began to question her. I asked her what other drugs this guy did. She said that she had seen him do cocaine while driving. They were at a red light and he did it on his arm. My mouth flew open! I was saddened. I asked her,

"Haven't you had enough of that? You are dating someone that acts almost like our dad. Why? What's wrong with you?" I asked. "He looks violent and out of control. You are too young for this type of life. You are better than this," I told her. "Clara, I am sorry,"I said, as I pointed in his direction. "You can no longer see this guy. I didn't care if you live in my house or not, you cannot see him anymore." She looked at me with disapproval, but with compassion. "Okay," she said. I never saw him again.

I guess they stopped seeing each other because he was no longer giving her money. Clara found out that he was also living with other women. I was okay with whatever it took for her to stop seeing him. Clara had begun working at the Westin Hotel downtown Atlanta. She eventually saved up enough money to get her own place with a friend. She was doing well and I was proud of her. She worked a lot because she now had her own bills and a lot of other things that she needed.

I had given Clara my old bedroom set. I had had that bedroom set for 15 years. It was the first and only bedroom set I ever owned. It was time to let it go. The paint had started peeling away. I put bricks underneath the bed to hold it up from where the legs have been worn down over time. You could feel the springs in the mattress, so I would put mattress cushions on the bed to make it feel softer. I remember when my new bedroom set arrived. After the guys put it all together I asked them to take the old down to my sister's house. They smiled as they looked at what they were taking to my sister. We knew it was old and needed to be thrown away, but she said it beat sleeping on the floor. Plus, she would have somewhere to put her clothes - even though one dresser drawer was missing. The top drawer of the chest was broken on the inside, so we sealed it shut with the outside base to keep the look complete. We just couldn't use it for anything else, but there were four other drawers to use, and the big dresser and mirror were okay. The movers were afraid to touch it because the pieces were so fragile. They were worried that if it was moved again something else would probably break off. I was paying them to do this, so they proceeded to take the old bedroom set to her. She was glad to have it. She said her apartment was starting to feel like home and she was happy. This was her first apartment. I would visit sometimes to see how she was doing. I knew she smoked and drank, but when I came around she wouldn't. I told her that she was in hcr own place and I didn't have any control there, but she still wanted to wait until I left. She said it didn't feel right to smoke and drink around me. When I visited, I never stayed long -- I didn't want to intrude on her life, especially when her friends were visiting her as well. She was happy and I was too.

A couple of months went by and then Clara called me and said that she had lost her job. She needed a new job quickly because her bills were due and she didn't want to lose her place. I was a restaurant manager then, so I gave her a job. She came to work the next day. She didn't want to work for me again, but she didn't have a choice -- she needed the money. She told me that Mom had come to her asking to come stay with her for a while until she and my dad got back on their feet, but Clara said no. Clara said that she would lose her place before she would live under the same roof with our dad again. I told her that Mom could help her get her bills caught up, but she didn't care. Clara's patience was a lot different than mine, but I remembered that at that age I was the same way. Mom had asked me the same question a year before that and I said no because I didn't want to deal with Dad either. So I had to understand when Clara said no.

A year later, Mom asked me again if we could get a place together until she got back on her feet. I looked at her, took a deep breath, and I said okay. I hoped it would take away any bad luck curse I had on me. When Mom came to me the first time I immediately said no. I had forgiven them for a lot of things, but I wasn't ready to deal with my father's ways - especially when he was drinking. I was grown and on my own and I had come too far emotionally to be disrespected that way again. Hell, I was in my own house and I paid the bills, so I wasn't going to be anybody's bitch, and I wasn't taking an ass whipping from no man - especially my father. God had spoken to me, but I didn't listen. "Honor thy father and thy mother," said God. "I will reward you. Trust me, Marilyn, and I will provide for you." I tried to shake His voice. I even went back to read that Scripture because I knew there had to be something in there that said if your parents mistreated you, you didn't have to honor them later. I was wrong. In the Bible, Exodus 20:12 says, "Honor thy father and thy mother, so that you may live long in the land the Lord your God is giving you."

I was really confused, but at that time I just ignored the voice. I had enrolled myself in college and had been going for a few months. My grades were good and I was starting to feel that my life was improving. I felt intelligent and important because I was accomplishing goals that I had set for myself a few years back. All of a sudden, within weeks, I was evicted from my apartment for vandalism and I lost my job. I had been there for almost four years and suddenly it was gone. I could not blame anyone but myself - I did things that I wasn't proud of: I gave free food to my friends. Managers and I would borrow money from the safe and put it back before the district manager came to visit the restaurant. Employees would work off the clock when they were close to getting overtime. Overtime was not allowed so I would give them extra time off during the week. I had everyone drive through the drive-thru to help the clock average show that we were moving the cars through the line by the target time. Some days when it was slow I would have an employee ride continuously through the drive thru until we made our target time. I was never at home and I paid rent on time so I didn't understand why I had to move. It was Clara. While I was at work she would be outside drinking with friends, making lots of noise and disturbing the neighbors. We argued a few times about her behavior. Clara decided it was best that she did not move with me to the next apartment. I didn't like it but I had no choice and I only had a few weeks to pack. Uncle Gerald was able to come stay with me to help with my son. I quickly found another job working at a grocery store. The pay wasn't great, but it was a job. There were times I would have Clara come to the store to get groceries. I would have a buggy full and I would only ring up half of it. Within a few months, I was fired from there. I started working again, this time at a dollar store, but I was not happy with the job either. I didn't like the work hours and I definitely didn't like the pay. I knew I wasn't going to be there long. While I was there I was able to get a lot of hygienic items and items that were damaged at a discount, I was enrolled in college so that gave me some encouragement. A few days later, I got a phone call from Clara saying that she had been in an accident in my car after dropping me off at work. She almost totaled my car. I lost my job because I didn't have a way to get there since my car was badly wrecked. I had to catch the bus to school. Catching the bus was difficult for me because I had not had to catch one in a while. I missed classes. I failed my first semester of school and was put on temporary probation. Everything in my life was turning upside down. I found another restaurant job near my parents' house. They helped me get back and forth to work for a while. My dad's patience wore thin when it came down to using his car, so I knew I had to hurry up and get my car fixed. Within a few weeks I was able to save up some money and get my car fixed. Luckily I had some friends that worked at a car collision shop and they were able to give me a great deal. After having my car in the shop for two weeks I was riding again. It couldn't have come at a better time because my dad had gotten on my last nerve complaining about having to pick me up and take me home. He didn't believe in putting a lot of miles on his car. I lived twenty minutes away and he was acting like I lived out of town. I would always make sure I put gas in his car and I gave him a little extra for himself. He still managed to have something to be irritated about when it came down to his car. It wasn't even new. He drove an early model four-door Plymouth that was bought from a friend that fixed up old cars and sold them at a cheap price. My parents needed something to drive to get them around town and to work. I understood he didn't want to damage his car because they truly depended on it, but was all that aggravation necessary? They were going through some financial hardship and Dad just wanted to take care of what he had until things got better.

They had to move out of their three bedroom house due to being behind on the rent. With little money and bad credit, Mom found a small one-bedroom apartment. They had to put most of their furniture in storage because the apartment was not big enough to hold all of their possession. Mom said the apartment was very dirty on the inside and smelled awful. Bugs were everywhere. Mom cleaned and cleaned - wiping down walls and pouring bleach down the drains in the kitchen and bathroom trying to get the stench out of the apartment. She said it was making her sick to her stomach. She didn't want to use the stove to cook and could barely sleep at night. The apartment looked shabby and tasteless. Even though that apartment was unsatisfactory, it was the only thing they could afford at the time and it was close to her job.

Mom had come to me again with that look of desperation in her eyes. She said, "Marilyn, please help me just long enough for me to breathe a little." They needed help to catch up on their bills. My dad wasn't working, so all the bills fell on her. Whatever was going on in my life, I felt as though she had something to do with it. I felt because I ignored God the first time He stopped blessing me. Whatever it was, I wanted it to stop. I told my mother she could move in immediately if she took that curse off of me. Of course she had no clue what I was talking about. I agreed to allow my parents to move in with me, long enough for Mom to rest her nerves and to save some money to move into a better place when they were able to.

Things had change a little since the last time Mom had asked if they could move in. My uncle and his friend from work were both living with me now in my two bedroom townhouse apartment. My son and I shared a room together and I gave my parents the other room, while my uncle Gerald and his friend Ted slept on the couch downstairs. The apartment was already small, and I had just added two more people. I had to start looking for a bigger place fast. We agreed to find a house that was big enough for all of us. We looked at several houses in Union City and Fayetteville, but mom said no to all of them. The houses were either too far from her job or were too big. She worried that the upkeep of the house would be too expensive. Within a few weeks, I was able to find a house that we all could agree on. It was very easy to get into. I felt that God had His hands on everything that I was doing to get us into a place. I didn't have a lot of money, but that didn't seem to bother anyone I talked to.

Within a month we had moved into the new house. Clara wasn't living with us at that time, but she was with me when I found the house. I remember telling her that I needed to be in a house that gave me my own space. I knew living with my parents again wasn't going to be easy, so I needed a room that gave me my own world when I closed the door. This house was exactly what I was looking for. It had an enormous master bedroom that was on the opposite end of the house - away from Mom and Dad. It was perfect. It had two walk-in closets and a long bathroom with two sinks, a tub on one end and a shower on the other. This room was fit for a queen, and it was mine. Clara and I jumped around in my soon-to-be room like little kids that just ate a whole lot of candy, I was so excited and she was so happy for me. Clara and I had our differences, but we loved each other dearly and always wanted to see each other happy. I had her back and she definitely had mine. There were three other rooms to choose from so my parents picked the room on the other end of the house that had big bay windows.

After a few weeks of settling in, things seem to be going well. My parents were able to take things out of storage and bring them to the house. I didn't agree at first because I wanted to buy new furniture but Mom explained that the storage was costing them a lot of money. I knew I was going to regret it later, but I agreed. Dad tried to complain about anything he could but no one seem to be disturbed about anything he had to say. Dad tried to establish his house rules but we quickly told him that we were all grown and paying bills so his house rules were void. He was irritated because he had no authority. Dad didn't work and all we asked was for him to contribute by helping everyone get to work. He made that complicated. Dad wasn't dependable due to his heavy drinking and his over-the-top attitude. Most of the time he stayed in their room looking out the bay window. He could see a lot of what went on in the neighborhood from that window. I felt sorry for some of the kids in the neighborhood because my dad saw everything they did.

Clara was still living with her roommate Kate. She was stressing over her bills, but wasn't ready to let her apartment go. She continued to work as many hours as she could in order to catch up on her bills. She liked having her own place and was determined to do whatever she had to do in order to keep it. I supported her decision and I did whatever I could to help her. We had been in our house for about three months when Mom lost her job. Her brothers had been calling her constantly to come home to help out with their sick mother. Mom was stressing over that and really wanted to go. Since she was not working I told her to go ahead and take care of her mother and we would continue to take care of the house. Dad would be okay staying at the house with us while she was gone. I giggled a little and had a slight grin on my face. I knew my dad was going to catch it from us while my mother was gone. I wasn't going to cook every time he was hungry. He was going to have to do for himself. He couldn't bully us the way he did my mom. I worked long hours and sometimes I would hang out with some friends after work. It was funny to see my dad cook, clean his room and do his own laundry. He tried to start a few arguments but after we told him we would tie him up to a chair and put him in the garage he calmed down. Mom called occasionally to check on us and to make sure we didn't do anything bad to my dad. But for the most part Mom was very happy to be back at her home taking care of her mom.

On Clara's 21st birthday, while at work with me, she met Art Mann. She was on her break sitting outside in the playground area. She was sad because it was her birthday and she didn't have any money to party with; she had bills to pay. As Art was walking into the restaurant, he spotted her. He spoke to her and asked her why she was looking so sad. She told him why. The next day, he came back and brought her a $100 bill to cheer her up. An employee and I stared, wondering what he saw in her to give her that money. We knew he was our age but he showed no interest in us, so we laughed it off. We giggled, saying we guess he didn't like women his own age.

Clara and Art began to date. He was helping her pay her bills which made her very happy. Shortly after that, she began to come to work later and later. Her work ethics around the job had changed. She would always leave her hat or something at home causing me to fuss or loan her a hat or shirt until the end of her shift. After a couple of no-shows at work, I decided it was time to let her go. I called her and told her she didn't have a job with me anymore. We argued a little, but she didn't care and neither did I. I expected more from her. Her attitude was changing and I didn't like it. This guy was taking care of her so she didn't have to work.

I met him a couple of times; he seemed to be okay. He was always taking her shopping and buying her all types of things. I was a little jealous, wondering why I couldn't find a man like that. I asked her what type of work he did and she said that his family owned a business and he was a supervisor. He drove a nice truck so I assumed he made a little money.

Some time had gone by and I hadn't heard from Clara. I went to check on her and her roommate told me that Clara was living in Miami, Florida with her boyfriend. I was confused. She didn't tell me anything. "Miami Florida?" I said, "What is going on?" I went home to tell my parents. They were just as confused as I was. Finally, Clara called. She told us that she had been living in Miami with Art hoping to get a job there. He told her that jobs were easier to get in Miami. We were not happy with the decision she had made without telling us anything. She said she was only going to be there briefly - just long enough to make enough money to pay her bills.

I then began to question her about Art. I thought he had a job. She said he wasn't working with his family anymore, and the truck he drove didn't belong to him. He had been staying with his cousin and driving his cousin's truck. So I asked her what happened to all the money he had. She couldn't explain. I didn't want to fuss too much because she was too far away from me and I didn't want her to get mad at me and not come back at all. When she did come back, she found out that her roommate had ripped her off and they were losing their apartment. She then decided to go back to Miami with Art.

This time things did not go so well with them. They got into an argument and she called me and told me he hit her. I spoke to him and he said it was an accident. She was getting out of the car and the door hit her in the face. I didn't care, I just wanted her home. I begged him to send her home. I even threatened to call the police on him if I had to.

After things had calmed down, she called back and told me she was okay and that she was catching the bus back home. When Clara arrived, her face still wore the bruise from their dispute in Miami. I was very upset about that. She continued to explain that it was an accident and more her fault than his. I was uncomfortable with what she said, but I was going to be there for her no matter what. After a few days of Clara being home, I noticed that they were on the phone together everyday, all day. Everywhere she went she had that phone on her ear. I didn't make a big deal of it until Clara had to come tell me that my grandmother died. I had just gotten in from work and began to wind down and relax around the house. Clara followed me and told me she had something to tell me. She looked at me and softly whispered that our Grandma had passed. I asked her what she was talking about. She took a deep breath and stated that my mother had called and told them that Grandma had passed and she wanted Clara to watch over me once I was told the news. I didn't believe her, so I called my grandma's house. My mother answered and I asked to speak to my grandma; she said I couldn't because she had passed away. I refused to believe what my mother had just said, but the tears began to flow rapidly down my face. I screamed because I didn't want it to be true. I missed her already. I didn't get to say goodbye. The truth is, I never wanted to. My heart wasn't ready to face the reality, but the pain was so real. Grandma had been sick for a few years. I would drive home on the weekends to visit with her as much as I could. I would always have a gift for her every time I visited. I brought wigs, shoes and dresses so that she could wear something new whenever she was able to go to church or just take a ride for some fresh air. The smile she would have on her face when she saw me was very optimistic. As time progressed, Grandma was becoming weaker and could barely get out of bed. She was losing weight and forgetting a lot of things. I was grateful that my mom and aunt were there to take care of her. I always prayed that she would get better or that God will give me a little more time with her. I cried all night. I wanted to go home so badly and see my grandma for one last time - to tell her that I loved her and missed her so much.

I didn't go to work that next day but I went a few days later just to make sure that everything was okay before we left to go to South Carolina to say our goodbyes. Mom was already in South Carolina she needed me to bring clothes for her as well as to make sure that everyone had what we needed for grandma's home-going service. So I had to do some shopping. Clara went with me for I was in no shape to do anything. I cried in every store we entered. At times I had to sit down and breathe from the pain I was feeling. As much as I loved to shop, this was a hard time for me. I couldn't stop thinking about my grandmother.

I called Clara to help me shop, but the whole time she was on her phone talking to Art. She hung up once to help me, but within five minutes he was calling back. As we continued to walk through the store, she would lose signal on her phone -her calls would drop, and he would call him right back. I showed her things to give her ideas, and her phone kept ringing, interrupting what we are doing. I was furious. I grabbed her phone and began to yell at him. I told him that I didn't appreciate how he was disrespecting our family in our time of grief. I needed my sister and he was being selfish by not allowing her to help me. He apologized and said he would call back later.

The next morning I went to work. It was 5 a.m. and I had asked Clara to drop me off so that she could use the car to run some errands. In the car, Clara was laying her head against the passenger window with her eyes closed, so I thought she was asleep. When we arrived at my job, we were getting out of the car and I noticed that she had been on the phone the whole time. I don't know what came over me but I was extremely mad. I snatched her phone out of her hand and began to curse him out. I couldn't believe that he had her on the phone at 5:00 in the morning not allowing her to get some rest.

Clara was mad at me for doing that. We got into a yelling match. She said it was her phone and I didn't have any right to take her phone and yell at her man. I didn't care, I was just mad. I decided not to give her my car to drive back home. She left anyway. She caught the bus home. A few hours later I calmed down and called her phone. I didn't get an answer. I called several times and she never picked up. I knew she was still angry, so I decided to try to talk to her when I got home. When I arrived at home later that evening I noticed she wasn't there. I asked Dad where she was and he said she had gone back to Miami. I was angry and hurt. We, as a family, were supposed to be leaving for Grandma's funeral and because of an argument between us Clara left. She was supposed to drive us to South Carolina.

My nerves were so messed up that Mom had asked Clara to drive because she didn't want me to, but then she just left. Wasn't that Clara's grandma too? I just couldn't believe it. Wow, she just left and went back to him like we didn't matter. Determined to say my goodbyes, I strengthened up enough to drive to South Carolina. We arrived early Friday morning in just enough time for me to go with my family to view Grandma's body before everyone else at the wake.

I walked in and I saw her lying in a beautiful pink casket. My tears were coming down so fast that I was wetting up her coffin. I was in disbelief. My grandma was gone. Words could not describe the way I was feeling. Seeing her lying there lifeless, I didn't want to let her go. My mother knew I was going to take her death hard because we were so close. I used to go see her every chance I got, bringing her gifts and much love, hoping to cheer her up as she went through her sickness.

Before grandma had gotten sick she would come visit us in Atlanta. We would always go shopping together to find some "Sunday suits" that she could wear to church when she went back home. We had so many fun times and memories and I was missing her dearly. The day of the funeral, my stomach ached. The clock was ticking as we all got dressed. The day before I had to be carried out of her wake services; I was crying so hard that I was hyperventilating and gasping for air. My niece, Mekca, sat next to me. She was taking it hard too, but she handled it better than me. It was hard to just sit there and look at her. I sat on the front row and all I could do was stare at her. It hurt; it hurt a lot. I had to be taken outside by several people and I was finally taken home and sent to bed for the rest of the day. The next day came and the time for the funeral drew near. I tried to stay busy by running errands and doing last-minute things. I remember stepping out onto the front porch to catch a bit of fresh air. I looked to my right, and there was the dreaded limousines coming towards our house. I ran back inside and hid in the back bedroom. I hated seeing those cars; they always spoke death of a loved one. When I saw them I knew someone was grieving the loss of someone special in their life. I managed to pull myself together, then we came together in prayer and proceeded towards the limousine to head to the church.

So many people had gathered to say their goodbyes. There were a lot of sad faces but none as sad as mine. When my mother and her brothers and sister went up to close her casket I ran behind them yelling, "Wait! Please let me close it with you." I had to see her one last time. I tried to keep it together but it was too hard for me to do. Family kept trying to keep me calm but I just wanted to cry. My grandmother had left me and gone home to Jesus. I wasn't finished showing her the woman I was growing into. There was so much of me that I wanted her to see.

As we drove to her burial site were my grandfather lay, my feelings of brokenness continued to pound me. That was the longest ride ever but it gave me a chance to calm down. I am from Estill, a country town in South Carolina, where there are lots of long dirt roads, woods, and farmland. We drove the back way around town to a deep part of the woods that I would never be able to get to again if I went by myself. The cars finally stopped and we all got out. We were at our family cemetery. My grandfather had passed a couple years before my grandmother, so to see his grave again brought back tenderness to my heart.

I was happy that my grandmother was united back with my grandfather, but it still hurt that she was gone. As they began to place her coffin in the dirt, my heart sank. The pain came all over again. I had to sit there as they covered her coffin with dirt. It hurt so badly. I cried so hard that people started coming towards me telling me to be strong and that my grandmother wouldn't want me to get sick behind her passing. They kept telling me she was in a better place, and maybe she was, but I didn't want to know that because I didn't want her to go. Grandma died from a blood disease which causes her to have kidney failure. Her body had slowly deteriorated away until she was just skin and bones. Mom had told me that she was in a better place and that her suffering was over. Knowing that Grandma was in God's hands now gave me a little peace but, for that moment and months later, all I could do was cry.

A month later, Mom came back home. She had been gone for a few months to help take care of Grandma before she passed. I was truly happy that my mom was able to be there to take care of her mother until her last days. Before we moved in together, it was almost impossible for my mom to go home to care for her mother because she was the only person working and their bills were so behind. Dad was between jobs and drinking a lot; therefore, he gave no support around the house. I couldn't imagine not being able to take care of and spend time with your mother knowing she may only have a few months to live. I hope that it gave Mom some peace to be there for her mother the last few months of her life.

After a couple of days after Mom had returned and everyone began to settle in; Mom felt that someone was missing – Clara. Clara had lost her apartment and was living pillar to post with her new boyfriend - sometimes in Miami, where he was from, and sometimes in Atlanta. They worked odd jobs to make money. I still wasn't on speaking terms with Clara at that time, so I didn't know anything unless Mom told me. Mom was very uncomfortable with Clara's living situation. She asked the family if it would be okay if we offered the two of them a place to stay. Because we were not on speaking terms at the time, I grudgingly agreed so my mom wouldn't be stressed further.

Eventually they moved into our home and things seemed to be going okay. Clara and I had started talking to each other again. They both were looking for jobs and planning their futures. Art Mann quickly became part of our family. We called him by his nickname, "Toonie". He was very easy-going and polite. While looking for a job - which was a struggle for him - he would help out by driving our mom to work at 6:00 every morning and helping out a lot around the house – whatever we asked of him. Clara eventually found a job at The Omni Hotel as a mini-bar attendant. I was definitely happy that I was no longer the only breadwinner.

Besides the fact that Toonie was a lot older than Clara, things seemed fine on the surface. We never heard them fighting - nothing more than just petty stuff. What we didn't know, but later found out, was that he used to rob people for a living. He would observe different locations like restaurants, gas stations and other businesses and rob them at gunpoint when they were going to make their bank deposits. Clara knew this but kept his secret. During their relationship, he would text her constantly and even had threatened to kill her if she left him.

A year went by and Clara continued to only confide what was really happening to her to her closest friends because she knew if we found out we would have him kicked out. She didn't show any signs of unhappiness or frustration concerning her relationship. We argued a lot over house responsibilities, so maybe that's why I didn't see what was right in my face.

I eventually had to give Toonie a job as a cook at Popeye's where I was an assistant manager. The holidays were nearing and since he'd just started the job, he didn't have money to get my sister any Christmas gifts. As a big sister, I wanted to make sure my little sister always had presents under the tree. So we went out together and I bought those gifts for him.

He thanked me and agreed to pay me back when he could. We shared a lot of personal moments. I could tell he truly wanted a life with my sister.

A couple of months passed and then Art's mother died. This was in February of 2007. He went home to bury his mom and ended up staying for two months due to sickle cell sickness that placed him in the hospital for a few weeks. This time apart gave Clara the opportunity to think about the relationship she was in. With him gone, she was able to hang out with some friends. She met a few new people, even another male friend. She didn't give any details about this guy she had met, only to say that she liked him and was ready to let Art Mann go.

During their time apart, Clara realized that she liked her life better without him. So she broke off their relationship over the phone.

We didn't understand why, but we accepted her wishes. I was happy that she was making some positive changes in her life - even taking her job more seriously. She told me that she had joined the safety committee and was getting involved in areas that improved her work behavior. I was also proud that she was dating someone her age.

We agreed to let Art come back for a week to gather all his things. I explained to Clara that if she was serious about leaving him that she couldn't do certain things with him when he returned. I told her to let him sleep downstairs on the couch and to stop smoking with him. Well, she didn't listen. I woke up early, headed to work, and the both of them were sleeping downstairs on the floor hugged up. I shook my head and walked out.

They had been up all night at the neighbor's house across the street playing cards, drinking, and getting high. I had a lot going on at that time so I didn't have time to stress about what she was doing. I was preparing for my finals. My college graduation was a month away. I was looking for a new car to purchase and looking forward to planning my graduation party. And I had my own secret, I felt death was following me, so I was trying not to stress over things. I wanted to stop yelling so much to avoid having a stroke, heart attack, or anything that could endanger my life.

I had started a side business doing taxes. Between that, working, and school, I barely had time to rest. That changed quickly. Within a few days, I had lost my job. I was the happiest person alive at that time. My job had become so stressful and the long hours were truly wearing me down. My boss was harassing me all the time, so I was happy that it was over and I didn't have to travel so far anymore. I had time to spend with my son, study for my finals and – most of all – I was able to be at church on Sundays.

One Sunday evening, Clara called to be picked up from the bus stop. Art used my car to go get her. A few minutes went by before I received a frantic call from Clara saying that they had gotten into it at the gas station after he picked her up from work. He left her at the gas station and came straight to the house saying Clara slammed his arm in the car door and that his arm was fractured. I was angry; I wanted some answers from him. "Did you hit her?" I asked. He said she attacked him. He stated that he bit her in her back to get her to let his arm go. I didn't believe him, and I was going to get my sister and get to the bottom of this. He had to go and that was the bottom line. Clara arrived at the house with her best friend. She was very angry but didn't want to talk about what happened. She just said that she was going to stay somewhere else for a while. She said he was my problem now. She said she would be okay and asked me not to call the police and not to put him out.

I wish that Clara had told us what happened, because we would have helped her. Her best friend told me later that when the police came to the gas station Clara lied to them so he wouldn't go to jail. She told them that her ex-boyfriend had attacked her and she didn't know where he went. We didn't hear from Clara for a couple of days. That Friday, Clara came to gather some more of her clothes. I was upset about that. I felt as though she left her man at the house with us and she was not there to assist. And I didn't want to pay her portion of the bills because she wasn't there. When I asked her to stay and work it out, she said no. We went back and forth arguing about it and, finally, I asked for my key and she gave it to me. She had no intention of coming back to the house, even after he left. I was very bitter for a couple of days, but I started to calm down some after Clara sent me a text saying that she would still help with the bills. Later on that week, I received some shocking news. I was on the phone with some of my son's father's relatives. They mentioned that my son's father, Marco, was getting married. I stuttered a little as I asked them to repeat the statement that they had just made. They said it again as if I didn't understand what they said the first time. I paused the conversation, not allowing it to go any further because I wanted to make sure I was hearing what I thought I heard. I was in shock. I didn't believe it was true. We had been separated for some time, but Marco never mentioned he was engaged to someone nor had he at any point mentioned that he even had a girlfriend. They thought I had already known, so they were just as surprised as I was. I put them on hold, clicked over to call him, and he immediately denied what I heard. He told me that I shouldn't believe everything I hear. Then he went on to say that he was at work so he would to talk to me later. I clicked back over to his family and told them what he said. They were upset then and wanted to know what was going on.

We continued to talk for a few more minutes, but in my mind I was wondering who this women was and why I never knew about her. He always acted as if he wasn't seeing anyone and that he needed me in his life. I was in shock and just couldn't believe Marco was getting married. When was he going to tell me? And, wow, he was getting married before me! And all this time I was afraid to fully go on with my life because I didn't want to leave him behind. We had had our ups and downs, but in times of need I tried to always be there. Hearing he was getting married made me question what I had been doing with my own life. Why hadn't I tried to settle down with someone special? I could have been married by now; what was I waiting on? Most of the guys I dated were not the marrying type and I wasn't looking for a husband. Hearing that he was getting married made me look within myself even more. It opened up some old feelings. We had a son together.

"How can he just up and get married?" I wondered. I felt like he was leaving us alone. How foolish was I to think that we would stay connected based on our son? Who was I kidding? We barely even saw each other. He worked two jobs, so he didn't come around much. We would flirt and see each other from time to time, but we didn't show any signs of getting back together on a serious level. It hurt to find out that way that he was getting married, but I knew he wasn't the man for me. I was jealous and afraid of what I was about to encounter. I had never seen him with another woman, and my son was about to have a stepmother. I wasn't prepared for that. I didn't even know what she looked like and I didn't know if we would get along or not, nor did I want to. I was so hurt that I paced the floor for hours hoping that his family was wrong and he was going to clear it up. If it was true, I knew eventually the truth would come out and I was going to have to deal with it, ready or not.

The following Sunday, Art Mann came to church with me. It was a good service, so good that he decided to join the church and get saved. He vowed to turn his life around. He got up from where we were sitting and walked up front to the altar and shook the pastor's hand. Then the deacons escorted him and others to a room to gather their information – their first steps on their new journey in Christ. He came out of that room with a smile on his face as if he was proud because he had chosen to give his life to Jesus. I was proud too because I had brought him to church for the first time and it changed him - at least I thought it did.

Later on that day, Art Mann came to me and asked me if I thought my sister would ever come back to him. I told him I doubted it. She was young and just wanted to hang out with her friends and enjoy life. Clara wasn't ready to settle down and she was still trying to establish a life of her own. He said he understood and that he would be moving on with his life. He asked if he could come back and visit us from time to time. I said he could always come visit and that he better come back for my graduation party. He said he would definitely be back for my graduation. He was leaving on Saturday. He had agreed to assist me with looking for a new car and in return I would give him my old car to drive back to Florida. He had a lot of things to travel with, so having a car would have been much easier for him. My current car was so old and beat up that I didn't mind him using it. I just hoped it would make it to Florida. While he was still at the house, he had agreed that on Wednesday after I came home from school we would go out looking for a new car for me.

Tuesday, April 3rd, 2007 was an ordinary day . . . or so I thought. I was awakened by Art Mann asking me if I was going to school early. I said yes; it was final exam week and I wanted to go study with some of my classmates at the school library to prepare for my exams. I was no longer working my stressful job, so I was able to invest time to make good grades for finals. By the time I had gotten up to get ready for school, Art Mann had already taken my mom to work, come back home to take my uncle to work, and dropped my son off at school. My father, Art, and I were the only ones left at the house.

Art Mann was in a good mood that morning. He was preparing to move back to Miami, Florida that Saturday and he was trying to take some pictures of me to show his family back home. He said he wanted his family to know how pretty I was. He said he was very proud to have us as his family and he wanted his other family to see who we were. So I happily posed for the pictures and went on to school.

I had two classes that day and I had to make sure that every day counted. I wanted to get some good time in with my study groups. I was excited because we were studying for some hard classes and I had help from other students. We were all determined to do well on our finals. We studied an hour before class and immediately after our Accounting II class. I proceeded back to the library to study again with my classmates. We had been studying for about thirty minutes when my cell phone started ringing. I didn't know the number so I didn't bother to answer it. The number continued to call my phone, so finally I stepped away from my study group and went to the front doorway to answer the call. It was my sister. I was stunned because she was calling me from a different number. I asked, "Where is your phone?" She said that she had left it over her friend's house. She said that she was at work and that Toonie was calling her job. She was worried that he could get her fired if he didn't stop calling her there. She asked me to talk to him and to ask him to stop calling her job. I was stunned because he had never called her job before - at least that's what I thought.

We hung up. I immediately called him; he was using my father's cell phone. No answer. I called again and still got no answer. So I called the house and asked my dad where Toonie was. Dad said he wasn't at the house and that he had given Toonie the car to go run some errands. Dad said that Toonie was supposed to have come back in less than thirty minutes, but that was over two hours ago.

My heart ached a little; I was scared. Something didn't feel right. My sister started calling me again. I told Dad that Clara was on the other line and I would call him back. We both agreed that she needed to call the police and we would be looking out for him. I clicked over to talk to her. She was frightened and a little worried. She said he was at her job and that her human resource department was paging her to come down because she had a visitor. She knew it was him. I told her to hang up the phone and call the police. I was scared too, so I started pacing the floor at the library. I couldn't study with my group, I couldn't focus. I was waiting for her to call me back and tell me that she was okay. I didn't know what else to do other than wait on her call, so I walked around with nervously waiting for her call. I just needed to know she was okay.

I waited and waited and waited. Everyone else seemed to call but her. I couldn't talk to anyone because I didn't want to miss her call. I kept stating that I couldn't talk because I was waiting to hear back from my sister. I told them that her crazy boyfriend was on her job and I was waiting to hear that she was safe. She never called, so I began calling her back. I got no answer. I called again and still no answer. I began to worry even more.

Finally one of my friends who I just got off the phone with called me back. He told me he had something that he wanted to tell me but he needed me to go home. "No, I can't go home," I said. "I'm waiting for my sister to call me back and I want to be nearby if she needs me to come pick her up from work." He asked me again to go home, and again I said no. I told him whatever he had to tell me that he was going to have to tell me over the phone because I wasn't going anywhere.

So he was left with no choice. He took a deep breath and told me that he was watching TV and his show was interrupted by some news about a shooting at the CNN Center. He told me to call up there to make sure the story was true and to make sure that my sister was okay. As soon as I hung up the phone with him I began to call her job. I was trembling badly and my heart was pounding hard.

After dialing the wrong number a couple of times, I finally got the operator at her job. I started talking fast: I asked if my sister was okay and if it was true that there was a shooting at their job. The operator said yes. I asked if it was my sister. She tried to put me on hold and somehow the phone hung up. So I called her back. I told her who I was again and I wanted to know if my sister was okay. Did something happen to her? I begged her not to put me on hold again. "Please!" I begged. She promised she wouldn't and she passed the phone to her supervisor. The supervisor got on the phone and softly told me that my sister had been shot. I screamed and asked if she was okay or if she was dead.

The lady told me that my sister had been shot and that she was being rushed to the hospital. I thanked her and ran to my car. I didn't have a clue about what I was supposed to do next. I panicked. I called my dad. He was so far away. He was at home and I was close to the hospital. My mom was at work, so she wasn't that far from me. I drove to her job to tell her what had happened. I didn't know how to tell her but I knew I had to tell her. Driving to her job wasn't easy at all. I felt numb. I was speeding and nervous and I'm very shocked that I didn't run into anybody or anything. As I arrived at her job, I stopped at the Human Resources office first to tell them the bad news. I knew that once I found my mother I had to tell her what had happened to Clara and she was not going to be able to say anything to anybody. I approached my mother. She smiled at me but changed her look quickly. She knew something was wrong because I had showed up on her job. My eyes were red so she knew something was really wrong. I slowly told her that Clara had been shot. She was shocked; she couldn't believe what I was saying. I couldn't believe what I was telling her myself. We rushed to the hospital to see Clara to make sure she was going to be okay.

Detectives and policemen had started calling my phone and they were also rushing me to come to the hospital. I wanted to get there as fast as I could. I just needed to see her face. I wanted to see her eyes. I needed her to look at me! I just needed her to look at me to confirm that she was going to be okay. I knew I still had to go get my father. I was going to go as soon as I finished with the detectives at the hospital and seeing my sister.

As Mom and I drove there we were debating back and forth on what my sister was going to say. She never wanted Toonie to come back from Florida when he left to bury his mother. We told her that she was wrong and that she had to at least allow him to get his belongings from my house. He had been staying with us for over a year and it was the right thing to do. We never saw this coming. WOW!!!! Mom and I smiled because we knew Clara was going to fuss at us about that. We felt bad, but we were only trying to do right by him as well as teach her they proper way to end a live-in relationship. We wanted him to leave feeling love from our family. Mom and I decided that whatever Clara had to say, we were not going to debate with her about it. We just wanted to make sure that she was okay.

We arrived and I ran to see her only to be stopped by the attendants at the front desk. They said that they were going to send someone out to talk to us. I didn't understand. I was upset. I wanted to see my sister. "Why can't I see her?" I asked. I was told to sit in a private room and someone would be out to talk to us as soon as possible. As I paced the floor, I started calling family and friends to tell them that Clara had been shot and that we were at the hospital waiting to see her. Minutes went by and I still hadn't seen my sister. "What's the problem?" I asked. I still didn't get a straight answer. Clara's friends began to arrive.

Then I got mad. "Why can't I see my sister?" I asked again. The lady at the front desk was on the phone calling for someone to assist me. Finally the doctor came out. She had a crowd of people with her. I charged at her. "Please take me to go see my sister," I begged her. She looked at me with sadness in her eyes. They asked me to sit down; I declined. I stated that I just wanted to see my sister.

The lady doctor then sat across from my mother and began to tell her that Clara had suffered two gunshots to her chest and she didn't make it. I started to scream. As soon as I heard two gunshots to the chest I knew she was dead. I ran. I was running into a brick wall and I didn't care. Somehow I was caught by one of the ladies that had come in with the doctor. I screamed and I screamed. I just couldn't believe that my sister was gone. I had been waiting there all this time thinking that she was going to be okay. I didn't know that they were preparing her body to be viewed by us. I couldn't believe it, so I asked to see her.

As they took us back to her room, family and friends were waiting in disbelief. They were more than angry. They wanted revenge. We were told that Art Mann had shot himself and that he was in the same hospital; he had just gotten out of surgery. He had shot himself in the head and was in critical condition. I truly didn't care about him, I just wanted to see my sister.

We approached her room. I opened the door. Her eyes were open. I walked in slowly, smiling. For some reason I just felt as though she was going to be okay. She slept with her eyes open so I just figure she was resting. I knew what the doctor had told me but I didn't want to believe it. I walked up to her. I began to talk to her as if she could hear me. There was a tube still in her mouth and I could see a spot of blood on the cotton that was around it. The doctors had cleaned her up and covered her up so nice that it was hard to tell she was gone. As I looked around the room I noticed there wasn't any machine or anything hooked up to her. I didn't hear any beep-beep noise coming from anywhere; she was just lying there asleep. They had taken her to another room to be viewed by us. I began to get nervous. I began to rub her face and touch her arms. Her body was getting cold. That's when it hit me. My sister was dead. I couldn't bring her back. I was hoping that I could be like the Charmed Ones and touch her and heal her body the way Leo did when an "Innocent" was badly injured. I was hoping that if she just heard my voice then maybe she would come back. I was having a bad nightmare and I wanted to wake up from it. The only problem was, I was awake! My body was numb. I was at a loss for words. I didn't want to accept her destiny. I felt as though God had made a mistake. "Why?" I pondered. I didn't understand.

As the nurse prepared to take Clara away, we had to gather ourselves and prepare to go home - leaving her behind. A couple of Clara's closest friends were there. One in particular, Crystie Owenie, took it really, really hard. She was screaming, and her mom had to escort her home as she was making herself ill. I walked around in circles with no sense of direction trying to get to my car from the garage to go home.

A detective walked with us to make sure no one was after us, especially the press. We were told someone would come to the house for us to identify Arthur Mann. A few hours went by, and then a detective finally arrived. I didn't understand why we had to identify him when they already had him in the ICU at Grady Memorial Hospital in critical condition. I guess they just wanted to confirm his identity and to find out why he did it.

It was an emotional night for my family, but one by one we went out to talk to the detective in his car answering every question he asked. He even had a picture of Art Mann that he showed us to confirm his identity. As I stared at the picture, I was in disbelief that someone who seemed to be so nice and caring would do something like this.

Once I left the detective's car and got back in the house, I walked up the stairs to my room. I lay in bed hoping I would get some understanding of what just happened. I never did. Day after day my phone would ring with family and friends calling to ask the same questions over and over. It angered me at times because I would have to repeat it over and over. Sometimes it would be someone from the same house or a friend that could have called one of our mutual friends. I knew they saw it on the news, so why would they call me for more details? It just upset my family and me even more.

Chapter 10

My Last Hello

The time had come for us to look at you and touch you for the last time. I didn't sleep at all the night before, hoping I could slow the clock down so I didn't have to say good bye to you. Morning still showed up on 119

time. I tried to do a lot of last minute things so I could stay busy. My stomach was in knots. I was shaking a lot and trying to hide it from my parents because I knew they were barely holding on themselves.

Uncle had taken me to the store to get a few things, and on our way back there were two limousines in front of us driving fast. My heart jumped. I was hoping they were not going to my house, but of course I was wrong. Trying to stay strong and hold back as many tears as I could, I rushed inside the house to make sure everyone was dressed and ready to go when the time came. We had an hour to get ready. Phones are ringing and everyone was asking the same questions over and over, "What time are we lining up?" "What time do we need to be at the church?" "Have the people from the funeral home arrived yet?" "What colors are we wearing?" My nerves were bad at this point and I was irritated. They should be here already or at least on their way and everyone that's supposed to be here is running late! The flower girls were not there to put on their corsages and I couldn't seem to get dressed; actually I just didn't want to. I needed everything to be perfect.

I had friends that were there just for me if I needed them, but I didn't know how to even ask for help. I didn't want to stop and think about anything - I just wanted to keep busy. I asked for someone to keep water and aspirin in her purse just in case I needed them. "And if I lose it in the church," I told them, "no matter what - don't take me away." I made everybody promise.

The time had come for everyone to get into their cars. We gathered at the bottom of the stairs and said a prayer. As we began to walk toward the limousine, my heart started to pound harder. My eyes watered, but I was trying so hard not to cry because everyone was depending on me. I sat up front with the driver, and I couldn't even hide the tears rolling from my eyes. The driver was talking to me a little - asking for directions and just holding conversation hoping to ease my pain. I was so nervous, I wondered whether I was going to pass out the moment I saw Clara. Will I be able to let you go?

We pulled up to the church and there were so many people standing outside that I was in disbelief. It felt like we were in a parade and people were waving and calling our names. Family and friends came from all over to show their support and it meant so much to me. Flower girls were showing up as we were walking into the church, so all I had to do was to make it inside. I could handle everything else but this.

The doors opened and it was my turn to enter the church. Mom and Dad were in front of me. My legs began to buckle and my tears were heavy. I wanted to leave, but I couldn't.

The usher had to help me walk down to you. It hurt to see you lying there like that. I tried to smile a little because you looked fabulous -- your favorite colors were blue and white, and we honored you by dressing you with those colors that day. I wanted you to have the best of everything this one last time.

As they helped me to my seat, our brother was there waiting on us. He had already been there an hour waiting for us to arrive. Thadd had traveled all the way from Macon State Prison, with the help of some kind police officers that my pastor knew, so that he could be with us on that unbearable day. His presence was very much needed and I was glad he made it. I had been able to send him a suit to wear. It was too small but he managed to wear it with grace. I was sitting in disbelief. Dad seemed to be barely breathing. My brother, on the other hand, was amazed at all the people he saw. He was waving and smiling, glad that he was able to come. He told me to cheer up because I had done a good job and that he was proud of me. He could only stay for a couple of hours.

The time had come for me to close your casket. I hesitated at first, but then I took a deep breath and got up. I wanted to do this, I just need to give you rest in my spirit. I had to find a way to accept this. As I pulled the sheet over your face, it felt as though I couldn't breathe. I slowly began to close the casket lid. I screamed out, "Because of who You are I give her back to You, Heavenly Father!" I could barely make it back to my seat, but with the help of my brother and family I did. I kept looking down at the casket, wanting to go back and wake Clara up and take her home with us, but I knew they would stop me. Thadd begged me to hang in there; everyone was depending on me.

The choir began to sing songs I had requested to honor you. The first song was "In Harm's Way" by Bebe Winans. This song was so special because you'd sung it to me, letting me know how much you appreciated the love I had for you. You knew nothing could stop me from keeping you out of harm's way. I tried to praise God and thank Him for your life as much as I could with whatever strength I had. I was exhausted, but for the first time I felt some relief. It felt like the load I had been carrying all week just lifted off my back and I was able to stand up straight.

The time had come for Thadd to go. He hugged us all and waved to the crowd of people. Everyone clapped for him and cheered as his kids ran to him for hugs. My dad walked him out along with the prison guards. Dad probably needed some fresh air and this was the perfect opportunity to breathe for a minute. Next, the time had come for us to take you to your final resting place. I didn't want to go. I hate gravesites. I didn't want to see them put you in the ground and cover you in dirt the way they did Grandma. The ride was long and traffic was rough. We didn't have a police escort, which made it even harder to get to where we were going, but we made it.

As we prepared to get out of the car, Dad swung his door open and vomited all over the ground. He couldn't take it anymore. He had stomached all he could. I looked back a couple of times waiting on him and Mom to come sit with me but they never came. I nodded my head to my pastor to say that it was okay to start without them. I held my head down most of the time because this was where I didn't want to be. Did they really expect for me to say goodbye to you, right here, right now? I couldn't do it. I was not going to let them put dirt over you. I was not going to sit there and watch them lower you in the ground, taking you away from me. Ashes to ashes, dust to dust, I placed the first flower on your casket, then others came and did the same. I sat there feeling broken and lost; I had to go home leaving my little sister behind. What was I going to do now?

Chapter 11

The Struggle is Real

It never failed… ever since my sister's death, I had been sleeping with my television on. There was something about the noise that kept my mind occupied while I slept. Sometimes I fell asleep without making sure that my TV was on, but I could always count on my son to come in my room and watch TV. Even my parents knew to let my television stay on through the night. Mom would get so happy when she saw my TV off. She noticed it because she was also struggling with her own sleeping disorder.

Mom slept in my sister's room to get away from the noise of the TV in her room because Dad stayed up all night watching TV. He sat in his room looking out the bay window hoping that Clara would come home. He wanted to be the first one to see her coming down the street in his car.

Mom said that she could hear my sister's voice in her head while she slept. So she would wake up in the middle of the night, running back to her room only to return to Clara's room again. I don't know why she even went into Clara's room. It is not that I was scared, it's just that I know there are so many memories of her in that room that it would be hard for me to sleep in there. I could barely sleep in my own room without thinking that Clara was going to wake me up asking me for a ride to work. I would run into her room in the middle of the night to wake her up just to have girl talk, or to jump on her bed and wrestle her until she woke up and then I would run back to my room. I felt this chill run through my body. I woke up suddenly. My room was so quiet that I could hear my heart beat. I squeezed my chest so tight, hoping to stop the pain that I felt. Thoughts of my sister's funeral went through my head. Is she really dead? How are we going to live without her? I began to cry, "I want my sister back!" I wished that this was a bad dream that I just couldn't wake up from. Maybe she will come to me in my dreams if I try to go back to sleep. But the pain I felt was so severe that I couldn't ignore it. The ache in my heart was unbearable; at times I didn't think I was going to make it.

I asked God to help me, "Mend my brokenness. Fix this!" I pleaded with Him. "Help me understand why it has to be this way." I sang Byron Cage's song "Broken, but I'm Healed" to myself: "God can heal . . . He can deliver . . . He can mend your brokenness." I sang until I was all cried out and my pillow was drenched with my tears. I got up to wash my face so my mom wouldn't know that I had been crying. I then returned and cut my TV on and just lay in bed thinking about how I was going to survive in this world without her. I was living without my other half and it hurt so badly. The pain was so overwhelming that I didn't think I would survive. I was clueless about what to do next. Who should I call and where should I go? I wanted to go somewhere and just cry and close my eyes until she reappeared. I didn't want anyone to bother me. I didn't want to hear that everything would be okay because it wouldn't. How could anyone say that when my sister's life has been taken from me and I couldn't do anything to change that? Why must I care and act like I am strong and say that she is in good hands now when I wasn't, and haven't washed my hands of her? Why! Why I ask? I need to know why, I must know why! What if I don't get the answer that I am looking for? Am I doomed? What is to happen with me now? Am I supposed to try to live after this? Why me? What if I don't want to-- would I be wrong for that? Can I just give up like many other people do? Haven't I suffered enough? Is my life always going to go downward? Will I ever feel like I belong?

I thought God was my heavenly Father so why didn't He prevent this from happening? What did I do? What did I do so wrong that my heart had an ache so severe that I could hardly breathe? My soul was empty and every motivation and determination that I had in me had vanished, wiped out. I was empty. I could barely stand; could barely hold my face up. I didn't want to anyway; I didn't want to look at anyone, and I didn't want anyone looking at me. I was afraid that I might see my sister walking away from me - she wouldn't hear me call her name and she would just keep on walking. What if I saw her, but it wasn't her - just someone else that looks like her? I was going to go crazy if that happened. I just knew it. If I just continued to hold my head down, I wouldn't have to look at anyone at all and I wouldn't have to worry about mistaking anybody for her. I wouldn't have to look out and see if I saw her coming towards me. To be safe and to make sure none of this happened, I will just stay in my room and wait for God to tell me what to do to fix this tragedy in my life. Yeah, that's where I would be. In a room that I was so scared of when it got dark.

My first Thanksgiving without Clara, I went to the grocery store to get everything that we needed in order to make Thanksgiving dinner. I remembered paying for the groceries. I drove all the way home only to realize that I had left all the groceries at the store. Mom looked at me and asked if I was going crazy. I smiled and softly said, "I am already there." Nothing felt right. I normally loved going grocery shopping, but that time I just wanted to get it over with. I was happy to return to the store and the groceries. They were still in the grocery cart where I left them. As Thanksgiving Day drew closer, I felt my stomach tighten more and more. She wasn't going to be there and I didn't know how I was going to feel. I tried to be strong for everybody, but it was so hard. I was already so stressed out because I didn't have a job, the bills were behind, and I had to still keep going without her. This was just too much for me. I couldn't cry like I wanted to because I had to watch out for Mom. I didn't want her to know that I was losing my mind because I didn't want her to lose hers. I wanted to cook everything in the refrigerator and bake everything I could think of. I was trying to act like I was happy, but under the surface I was hurting all over. Normally, I would be doing all the cooking and Clara would bake all desserts. She hated being in the kitchen, but I would bribe her by making her a pan of dressing just for herself. Mom wanted to start four days early and I was dragging along hoping that the day would never come. I had the jitters, and I didn't want anyone to see me fall apart. Everybody thought that I was so strong, but did they really understand that he killed my sister? I was like a bowl of mashed potatoes: soft and mushy. Everyone is breakable and I was falling apart. My brother was in jail and my sister's body was in her grave. Every time I would say that word I would get chills all over me. I just couldn't believe that she was gone.

I cooked all her favorite foods: turkey and dressing, macaroni and cheese, and I even made some fried corn and fried cabbage for my brother -pretending that he would be there in spirit. He was in jail and I knew that he felt sad and all alone with no one to talk to. The void I was feeling in my heart I also tasted in the food. The dressing didn't taste the same. The sweet potato pies had cracked in the middle and I couldn't seem to get the cake to stay in place. Mom came and touched me on the shoulder and told me that everything was going to be okay. She said that if I didn't stop cooking she was going to medicate me and put me to bed. I was unstable; trying to hold on by cooking but it didn't go as planned. I did as mom asked and sat in the living room to calm my nerves. I thought to myself, too many people are missing: my brother, my sister, and Toonie -- the man that murdered Clara. We still somehow thought of him, remembering some of his good and of course the bad. Some of our memories of her involved him as well, so it was kind of hard to hate him all the time. Her birthday was coming up and I hadn't done anything that I wanted to do for her. November 27 - five days after

Thanksgiving. No wonder I was miserable. How could I be happy about anything when the person I lived for was gone?

I was very disappointed that I didn't do anything in her memory. I called most of her friends and I went to visit her grave with Mom, Dad, my uncle Gerald and my son, Macarion. I felt that if I could just hear her voice maybe I would feel better, or maybe I might just go crazy. Christmas was going to be horrible and I didn't care. I always shopped for her like she was my child. I got excited to play Miss Santa Claus. I never would get any gifts, but I always made sure that everyone else did. Since I was the oldest, it always felt good to give to everyone else. I felt honored to be able to bring joy to everyone in the house, hoping to fill everyone with the joy of Christmas. Money was low around the house; however, I still made sure we had a Christmas. My sister could always count on me to save the day. After she was gone, I wished that somebody would just save my day and take my pain away. But there was no comfort zone. The pain was suffocating me and I couldn't seem to get any relief from it.

It was hard for me to show my pain the way I wanted to because Mom and Dad were hurting so much. Mom needed me to be strong for her and she was really depending on me to help her through her pain. Mom, for a long time, had been dealing with a lot of stress from Dad drinking and his mental abuse. You would think that he would have calmed down because of my sister's death, but it only made things worse. He wanted to blame everyone else for her death. I knew deep down inside that he just felt guilty because of the type of relationship he had with Clara, and that was not able to fix it before she was killed. He felt as though everyone should grieve the same way he did.

I hated the way he bothered my mom with his complaining, whining, and foul language - like she really needed that right then. Sometimes I thought that wouldn't be satisfied until she went into a deep depression, lost her mind, and never came back. Why didn't he just leave since he was so unhappy? Mr. Miserable. Would my mother ever be happy? I hoped that she would be before she took her last breath in this cruel world.

My mother had worked hard to care for us. She was very giving of herself to others. She took a lot from people just to keep the peace. She had been hurt so many times and she deserved better. I couldn't take away the pain in her heart from losing my sister, but I would try to do my damnedest to help her through it all.

One Saturday morning, we got up and got dressed because one of our closest family friends were picking us up to come sit and fellowship with them for a while at their house.A breath of fresh air was definitely something we all needed. We had known them since I was a little girl, so it felt good to be around friends that were like family. I hadn't seen their kids since we were little, so I was looking forward to seeing how everyone was doing and how many kids they had. After a few hours of fun and much needed laughter we headed back to the house.

When we returned to the house I stopped to check the mailbox. As I started going through I mail, I saw a letter from Art Mann from Fulton County Jail. I ran into the house yelling to my parents. I had a letter addressed to me from him. I didn't want to touch it, so I took another piece of mail and pushed his letter out of my hand onto the table. Everyone gathered and stared at the letter like it was a foreign object. We were in disbelief that he had the audacity to write us. When did he even have time to write? I thought he was still at Grady Hospital in critical condition. No one had called us and told us anything. I felt a little frightened knowing that he was alive and out of the hospital.

Mom couldn't take it; she didn't even want to be in the same house with the letter so she left with her close friend. I continued contemplating what to do with that letter. The envelope looked as if it had been stored away for some time. It looked as if someone mistreated it but kept it for a day when they didn't have anything else to use and needed an envelope. That someone gave that envelope to Arthur Mann to use to write to me. The envelope had brown paper stains on it and rugged edges from not being well kept. I took a deep breath and reached to open the letter. I first began to read the outside of the envelope, where Art Mann had wished me a happy Mother's Day and a happy graduation. Wow, he had some nerve to even think that I would want to hear that from him. So I proceed to open it.

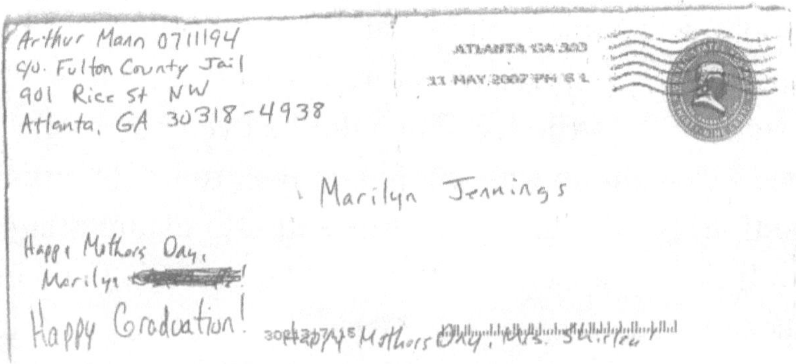

To Mrs. Shirley + Marilyn Jennings

I would like to start off by saying hello
I am very sorry for what happened
between me and Clara. Only God knows what
was going on and that I wish that I
had never gone that way. I am crying
out for help now because I have no more
eye, or jaw, and I have to use my
hand to talk. I am very sorry. Everyone
thinks I went to the CNN building
to kill my girl. Only God knows what
happened between me and her. I send
my love to the family. I ask God to
forgive me for having a gun in the house.
The only one who knew was Clara. When she
left she took the gun with her. When I
checked for it a couple of weeks later, I
knew she had taken it. I went to her job,
where she was. When I saw her. She said
to me. "Toon, if you love me, you will join m

I tried to take the gun back. I grabbed the trigger and it went off, shooting Clara. When the gun shot her. I shot myself in the head. I have seizures now, so I feel like I am going to pass any day. I have no family behind me. If anything happens to me I am not expecting you to have a funeral for me, but at least you can cremate me and put me next to Clara - the one I've always loved. May God forgive us for all of the things we have done in our life. I ask Mrs. Shirley and Marilyn to please forgive me. in the name of Jesus. for the sin we have comitted to one another. If you can find it in your heart, please send $20 or $25 postal money order so I can buy a sprite + a cake. Please lay me to rest

Later on that evening, while watching television, my phone rang and it was a three-way call from Art Mann. A lady asked for me, clicked him on, and he began to talk to me. I froze for a quick second; I couldn't believe he thought he could call me like we were cool, after what he had done. He said hello and asked how I was doing. "You killed my sister!" I yelled into the phone. "How dare you call me?" Before he could get another word out I hung up the phone. The lady that called for him rang me back to apologize for making that three-way call for him. I understood that she didn't know who she was making the call for, but it took a couple days before I could get over it.

Chapter 12

Face to Face with Tragedy

The time had come for us to go meet with the district attorney to discuss how we wanted to proceed with my sister's murder trial. I began to think back on our journey thus far. We had attended several bond hearings and the grand jury indictment hoping to see him in the courtroom, but we had no luck. We wore our "Rest in Peace" shirts so that everyone in that courtroom knew that we were her family. We were so nervous going to those courtrooms not knowing what to expect from reporters or anyone else. We walked close together at a slow pace silently praying for God to carry us through. Everything that we thought was going to happen didn't happen. Maybe that was God's plan. I wished Art would have just pleaded guilty so we wouldn't have had to deal with any of it again, but that wasn't the case.

A car came to the house to take us to meet with the district attorney and his staff. As we headed downtown to his office, our hearts began to break a little more knowing we had to talk about Clara's murder. I could feel the tears preparing to fall from my face the closer we came to the courthouse. We sat in his foyer for a few minutes waiting for someone to bring us in. This gave us a minute to gather our thoughts together and to shake off the nervous tension passing through us.

As we walked into his office, we were surrounded by the district attorney and some of his staff members. We were introduced to the prosecutor who would be handling our case, and advocates who would be assisting us with grief counseling and whatever support we needed. We felt welcomed. They looked into our eyes with great sorrow. We broke into tears instantly. The room was quiet for a few minutes while we tried to get ourselves together. We began to open up and get acquainted with everyone in the room. We sat at the round table and talked about our lives with Art Mann and our lives without Clara. Even they were confused about how much love we gave to Art Mann only for him to do something so heart-wrenching to our family. The district attorney told us that they came to the funeral, but didn't want to disturb us - they just wanted to be there for support and to observe. We then talked about the case. Art Mann was charged with first-degree murder. Surprisingly, this was not the first time that he had been involved in a murder case. A few years prior, he had served time for killing someone while committing a robbery in Florida. He was released on good behavior, but was later convicted for child molestation after conceiving a child with a minor. Because of his criminal history, Art Mann wouldn't be eligible this time for parole if he was convicted for killing my sister. That was a small relief for me. I truly didn't think that I could handle the idea of this man ever being released from prison again, and for "good behavior" no less. How does anyone even qualify for good behavior after they have killed someone - especially the way he killed my sister? The person they killed doesn't get a second chance at life so why should they?

The question was asked if we wanted to seek the death penalty for Art Mann. We paused for a minute, and Mom answered no. Dad and I agreed. As much pain as we were in, we did not have the strength to kill someone else. Besides, killing him wasn't going to bring Clara back. It would just prolong our time in court. We didn't want to wait years to go to trial, or sit through years of appeals. The pain was already unbearable, and a lengthy court battle would have mentally destroyed us. We would be at peace knowing that Art Mann would be in prison for the rest of his life.

After a few more questions and instructions, the driver took us back home where we would prepare for the next meeting. I wondered if Art Mann even realize that his life was in our hands. How grateful he should have been to know that God didn't create us with vengeance in our hearts. The love we had for him outweighed the love he had for us. Sadly, Art's actions left us with no strength and no desire to wake up to face our new reality day after day after day. Our reason for living was gone along with our purpose to move forward. We were in the hands of the Lord because we had no one else to turn to. We woke up only because God woke us up. Nothing else mattered after that. Many days we would lie in bed quietly waiting for the time to sleep more hours away.

The day of his trial finally came. I spent a few days prior making sure we had our clothes picked out for the week. We knew that there would be some media attention and I wanted to make sure that everyone was looking their best. My parents and I discuss that I would talk to the media when the time came. I had waited many months for that day. Many sleepless nights went by trying to understand why someone who we treated like family would do this to us. I felt as though we had a mysterious person living with us that we truly didn't know. I needed to see him again. It was hard to believe that this guy, who seemed to be so loving and kind, had killed my sister. I hadn't seen his face since that fateful day I left home for school, and waved goodbye at him, planning to talk again later that evening. In a way, I was somewhat afraid of him, and I dreamed of looking him directly in his eyes so that I could rid myself of the fear and see him for what he actually was: the murderer who put my sister to death. I was told that he shot himself in the face after he shot my sister three times. I tried to imagine what he was going to look like, but I couldn't and that bothered me deeply. I had to be brave. I needed to see him with his "new identity". I wanted to make sure he'd never walk past me and I didn't know his face.

We arrive a few minutes early. Sitting outside the courtroom with our victims advocate, Art Mann's attorney approach us. She politely introduced herself to us. She then gave my family her condolences and explained to us that she had to do her job as a public defender and asked for our understanding. She was a brown-skinned black woman, had a medium build, and was average in height. She wore business attire as an attorney would. She looked very smart and educated. Her presence was heartfelt so we nodded our heads with understanding. As ready as I was, there was a delay in me seeing him on the first day. His attorney had subpoenaed my mother and me to be character witnesses for him. I was dumb struck. How could they ask for such a thing? What did he expect me to say in his defense? I wondered those things the first two days of the trial as we sat outside in the lobby, waiting for the chance to sit and witness his trial in action. My dad was the first to be called and he had the opportunity to go in on the first day. At the beginning of the trial, the prosecutor requested that my dad tell what he had remembered on that day since he was the last person to see and speak with Art Mann before he left the house.

The prosecutor had prepped my father weeks before the trial. They knew my father was an alcoholic, and they wanted to make sure he did not drink the day before the trial. They had even discussed putting him up in a hotel to make sure he was sober when he was up on the witness stand. Little did the prosecutor know, my father had been waiting for this day to come for a long time! If he wanted to drink, he didn't. He was more ready to get up on the witness stand than he had ever been for anything in his life. "He took my baby," my father would say over and over as tears rolled from his eyes. He was more than ready to see justice for Clara and nothing or no one was going to get in the way of that.

This was a hard time for us all, but we were all prepared to face Art and to get some type of justice so we could move forward with our lives and, more importantly, to begin healing. While Mom and I sat outside the courtroom we notice that a few people from Clara's job had come to testify on her behalf, telling what they on the tragic day. On their way out they came over to my mom and me to introduce themselves. I was so thankful to have our advocate sit with us every day at trial. After the third day of the trial, my mother and I were finally allowed to come in. Art's attorney had decided against using us as character witnesses. I was so relieved. I didn't think I would have said anything if they would have asked me to. Most likely, my mother would have just cried her eyes out; not being able to get one word out. I was truly happy that they didn't call us at all - not even the prosecutor over my sister's case - as we sat there with our stomachs in knots, trying to hold on to what little strength we had in order to listen to what Art Mann had to say when his attorney called him to the stand.

As we enter the courtroom for the first time I felt a slight discomfort. The atmosphere in the court room felt cold and dark. Everyone looked so serious but yet sympathetic as we entered. There were a few cameras filming the proceedings of the case. Everyone sat quietly as the attorneys recounted the events that led to Clara's death. Clara's other best friend Crystie Owenie was there to see justice served. She was very angry and agitated sitting there waiting to hear what everyone had to say. I would have to calm her down at times, when it seemed that she would get heated from some of the explanations she was hearing from Art Mann's attorney. Clara and Crystie together were nothing to play with. They were tag team play-wrestling champions; they wasted no time putting people in check. They were prepared to fight at any given situation. They both had attitudes and smart mouths that always kept them tangled up in arguments with their peers. My son's father, Henry, came to court on that day as well to show his moral support, to see how things were coming along, and to see if we needed anything. He felt as though Clara was like a sister to him and he wanted to see justice served on her behalf. Henry's part-time job had been adjacent to Clara's job and they would see each other often on their lunch breaks. We were not together but Henry still loved our family and I was thankful for his support in our time of sorrow.

Initially, Art's attorney tried to paint the picture of Clara's murder as being an accident. She argued that Art had no attention of harming my sister. She was very aggressive in her argument. Judge James Bodiford quickly threw that out. He stated that the video showed Art Mann dragging my sister down the escalator by her hair - which certainly didn't look like an accident - with a gun in his hand that he never put away. The video also showed her pulling and struggling to get away from him. When Art Mann got to the bottom of the escalator, he stood over her and shot her three times before pulling the trigger on himself. None of it looked like an accident.

The judge was a white male, very mature in age. He had a head full of grey hair and didn't show any facial expressions. He seemed to have been a judge for a while and wasn't letting anything get past him. He was very impatient, and I could tell that he had a slight attitude. He looked very irritated, and I could tell he was ready to get this trial over with. He looked as though he was disgusted to have to sit and listen to that nonsense. That made me smile with relief. I was glad to know that this judge didn't have time for games or any last-minute proposals. For a split second, I was proud to know that my sister fought for her life to the very end. I knew that if he had not had that gun over her, she would have gotten away after getting in a few hits of her own. Clara had a strong personality and wasn't afraid of anything. Even though I was the older sister, Clara always felt that she needed to protect me from any harm or danger.

I remembered a time when a former employee said some mean things to me. I had been helping this employee with his community service and giving him hours on the schedule to make sure he could satisfy his probation. Clara knew this, so it angered her to know that he was talking to me like that. A couple of days had gone by, and on Clara's way home from work, she asked her friend to take her to my old job where this employee was still working. She found him and they immediately got into an argument. Clara then jumped over the counter and punched him dead in the face several times before leaving the building. She told him, "No one disrespects my sister and gets away with it!"

My mom was not happy about that, but we laughed and I felt good because Clara did something that I wanted to do. After Clara's death, that same young man came to our house to apologize to me and offer his condolences and support. That warmed my heart and I thanked him for being able to be a support to my family during our time of grief. He even wore a shirt at my sister's funeral with her image on it. There were several people who wore shirts with Clara's face on them to honor her, but the one that stood out the most was the one worn by one of Clara's best friends, Nikkia Gotter. It was a pink tank top with Clara's face on the front that had the words "Stop Domestic Violence" circled in red on the back. From that moment, something was birthed in my spirit. I knew I had to do something! There was no way I was going to be able to continue living life without my sister while waiting for someone else to come to my rescue to contain the rage, the unbearable hurt, and the over-powering nightmares that consumed me. I knew it was up to me to open a long-closed door concerning domestic violence.

As I sat in that courtroom, I wondered how deep into our lives Art Mann's attorney was prepared to go. What had he told them about us? Arthur Mann witnessed many fights between my mom and dad, and on several occasions my sister was there to jump in to help my mom fight our dad. Then there was the time when my father and sister got into it because he didn't want her sleeping in the bed that he had bought because she didn't share her last blunt with him. I remembered it like yesterday. It was late in the evening and were all trying to settle in. Dad was yelling throughout the house, and was trying to move everything that belonged to Art outside to the sidewalk.

We hadn't been living in the neighborhood very long, and I was embarrassed by the way my father was acting - putting our neighbors all in our business. We had to stop him. Clara, Art Mann and I, along with a friend, started bringing the furniture back in to the house. That really angered my father. He went to the garage and grabbed an ax handle and came toward my sister with it. I jumped him from behind so he couldn't hurt Clara.

Together, Clara and I slammed him on the ground, taking the ax handle from him. We then began stomping him with our bare feet, not allowing him to get up to fight us back.

Art Mann broke up the fight and my Dad was able to get into his car and drive off only to return shortly before sunrise feeling some type of way from the bruising we had given him. He went to his room, rested for a couple of days, and never brought the subject up again. That was the type of family we were: Never dealing with the problem at hand, pushing it under the rug, and never bringing the subject or situation up again. However, we all knew that once Dad started drinking again, he would be the first to bring up what was said or done to him but never what he did to anyone else.

As the trial went on, nothing concerning our personal lives ever came up. However, the prosecuting attorney, along with the district attorney of Atlanta, knew that we were a family that lived in the midst of domestic violence. As I sat in that courtroom staring at Art Mann I often wondered why he would hurt Clara since he had seen some of the things she had been dealing with. Did he feel any compassion or sympathy as a man dating her? Why didn't he see her as someone that was bruised mentally and needed a knight in shining armor to come sweep her off her feet and fill her life with much-needed love and compassion? Instead, he inflicted more pain on her while she was living and then he took her life. People can be so selfish and cruel.

When Art Mann, took the stand, I took note of his tan suit and tie, low haircut, (he was no longer wearing braids) and the innocent look in his one eye. He only had one because when he shot himself in the side of his chin, the bullet exited through his left eye. Even with that injury he looked very nice, almost as though someone had been taking good care of him. We could tell he was nervous and ashamed to look at us. We almost felt sorry for him but we were quickly reminded by our victim advocates not to be moved by anything he did because he could have just pleaded guilty and not taken us through the agony of a trial. Every time he looked toward us he would always see me staring at him. Crystie was in rage just looking at him. If her looks could killed, Art Mann's family would not have been able to identify his body. While sitting in that court room, I wondered if he went to the altar that Sunday with me knowing that he was about to kill my sister and he was asking God to forgive him. Art Mann's attorney did a good job of representing him. She focus on his current stage of depression during those times because his mother had just passed a few months prior. She made it seem that he was in pain and just need Clara to comfort him during his time of grief and Clara rejected him. She had me on the edge of my seat until the prosecutor got up to cross-examine Art Mann. This lady was very sharp. She wore a two-piece grey dress suit. She was a light-skinned black woman, kind of short, with a slender build. She had Art Mann stumbling over his words and at times he didn't have anything to say when she asked certain questions or revealed to him what he said in past statements. He was guilty and she knew exactly how to prove it. She even used illustrations that showed what took place. Art Mann didn't seem to be a victim once she cross-examined him. She made him look like the murderer he was. Both attorneys rested their cases that day and would prepare to give their closing arguments the next morning. We went home for the day, hoping that we didn't have to been in court all week.

We arrived the next day - a Thursday morning - preparing to hear the closing remarks of both attorneys. Crystie wasn't able to come and Henry had to go back to work. It was Dad, Mom and myself along with our advocate and a few people from the attorney offices.

As I sat and listened to his lawyer's closing argument, I felt she was trying to convince the jury that he was the victim and should be forgiven for what he did. That made me nervous a little. I had my fingers crossed and I began to silently pray. I wanted him to be put away for life. I felt a lot better when the prosecutor for my sister gave her closing statement. I was ready for the verdict.

The jury left for a few hours to make their decision. We all went to lunch while we patiently waited for the jury to come back. We ate at the food court near the courthouse. We were very nervous but tried to camouflage it by smiling and talking. As we headed back to the courthouse, we were told that the district attorney wanted to speak with us. We headed to his office where we were asked our thoughts about the trial and what our plans were moving forward. We said that we hoped for the best and only knew that we were doing things one day at a time. We all agreed that the lawyers that handled our case did a great job and we were just waiting to see what the jury thought. It was starting to get late, so I assumed we were going to have to wait until the next day. A few minutes before the court was to close, the jury came back with their verdict. My heart was beating fast. I was ready but I was afraid to hear what they had to say. Everyone entered the courtroom. It was a full house. People who were not there from the beginning came to hear the reading of the verdict. There were extra police officers standing in the courtroom to make sure no one got out of hand once the verdict was read. A police officer approached us and told us that no matter what the verdict he was, that we could not yell, scream or do anything that would cause bodily harm to anyone. If we felt that we could not keep calm, he suggested that we leave the courtroom before the verdict was read. We had no plans of leaving the courtroom. We gathered ourselves together holding hands - ready to embrace the verdict.

The judge asked the jury if they had reached their verdict and they responded, "Yes." The paper was then handed to the judge to view and then handed back to the deputy sheriff to read out loud in the courtroom. I took a deep breath as the deputy read from the paper. He said, "In the case, The State of Georgia versus Art Mann, on the first count of murder, we, the jury, find the defendant guilty. On count two: felony murder, we, the jury, find the defendant guilty. On the third count: felony murder, we, the jury, find the defendant guilty. On the fourth count: kidnapping with bodily injury, we, the jury, find the defendant guilty. On the fifth count: aggravated assault with a deadly weapon, we, the jury, find the defendant guilty. On count six: possession of a firearm during the commission of a felony, we, the jury, find the defendant guilty." The verdict was signed on the 27th day of February, 2008.

That was the day my family finally began putting that horrible thing to rest. As I sat there listening to all those guilty verdicts that I was so anxious and wanted to hear, I was happy, but I was dissatisfied. I still felt the pain of Clara not being there and knowing that he killed her.

The time was nearing for me to get up and speak on my family's behalf. I was so nervous I was trembling. Finally, the time came when I was called up. I walked up with my statement in my hand accompanied by a victim's advocate who had been with us through the entire trial. Her presence there with me helped a little. She was also there to help me speak to the judge if I needed her but I was determined not to break down so that I could say everything on my own that I needed to say for my mom, dad, brother, and myself.

As I stood in front of the judge I began to cry a little. I stated my full name. With hesitation in my voice I began to say, "Your Honor, I never knew pain like this ever existed until April 3rd when my sister was killed by Art Mann. I have always been there to protect her from harm, and that was the first time I wasn't there to save her."

The judge asked if Clara was my little sister; I said that she was my only sister. The day Art Mann killed her was the last time I heard her voice. I stated that the pain was so severe that I had to sleep with my television on so I could hide from the nightmares and from the darkness. A part of my life died when my sister left. I cried out that I didn't even know what my purpose in life was anymore. I had to pray every day for strength and courage so that I could continue my destiny. My six–year-old son didn't understand why his auntie was taken from him by a man that he called "uncle". We didn't call him by his real name, Art Mann, we called him Toonie, his nickname. My sister wasn't perfect, but she was my sister that God created for me, and Toonie, aka Art Mann, did not have the right to take her life. I stated to the judge, "These last few days, Art Mann presented himself to you in a suit to a jury of 12, fighting for his life. On April 11th, 2007, the day after my birthday, my sister was carried by six of her friends and family wearing a suit in a coffin because she was not given the opportunity to fight for her life." I stated that my sister at one time did love Art Mann. We gave them a place to stay because we loved her and grew to love him. She gave him her best when she gave him her family. Why couldn't he love her enough to let her go and live when it was time for their relationship to end?

I told him, "My father sits in his room window everyday looking down the street, hoping to see if his youngest daughter is going to come home in his car. My mom from day one embraced Art Mann like her own son. She cooked and fixed his dinner every day. They drank coffee together every morning on her way to work. Art Mann showed his thanks and gratitude by shooting my sister in the back of her head. My mother now walks the hall at night running from her nightmares and her broken heart. Art Mann told me he wished he had a sister like me. I gave him a job, I brought him clothes. I even rented cars for him to go home to see about his dying mother. I cared for him, and I wanted to do what I could to help him. He thanked me by shooting my sister twice in the chest and finally in her torso."

"I can't even look my parents in their eyes," I told him, "because it hurts so badly and it's hard to gaze beyond their pain." I told the judge I hoped that Art Mann's life turned out to be as unbearable as mine was waking up every morning without my sister. "Your Honor," I said, "I know whatever decision that you make on today will not bring my sister back, so there will be no justice for me. And as a taxpayer, I still have to contribute to his expenses while he is living behind bars. His family will be able to visit him and talk to him. I have to go to my sister's grave when I want to talk to her." I then told the judge that Art Mann didn't deserve to ever walk the streets again, where he would be given the opportunity to prey on another family as he had done to mine. I paused for a brief moment, and then thanked the judge for listening to what I had to say. I walked back to my seat feeling relief; I had been waiting for months to get that off my chest. I hugged my parents as I sat down with them to wait for the sentencing.

The judge then asked if Art Mann had anything to say. He hesitated at first; we could hear him talking to his lawyers, saying he didn't know what to say after what I had said. His lawyer suggested that he still get up and say something. With some doubtfulness in his face, he stood up and told the judge he just wanted to apologize to the family for what happened. No one was moved by what he said - especially not the judge who was quick to tell Art Mann that he was sentencing him to life in prison without the possibility of parole, and that was for both the murder conviction and the kidnapping conviction. Art Manning was then given an additional five years to follow for the firearm charge: possession of a firearm during the commission of a felony. With disgust in his eyes, the judge stated that it was a horrible thing that happened, and he hoped, that while in jail, Art Mann would think about what he had done. Court was then dismissed and we were free to go home.

There was a moment of relief in our hearts. We didn't have to face another day of looking at the man that killed our Clara. We thanked everyone that came out to support us. Hugs were being giving from everyone that witnessed the case. They had a lot of sympathy for my family and we appreciated it.

As we were escorted out of the courtroom, the news reporters were waiting to ask us a few questions. My parents and I decided that I would talk to the reporters and they would stand with me as I answered questions. For us, as a family, I stated that we were satisfied with the outcome and relieved that it was finally over.

The very next day there was another letter in the mailbox from Art Mann.

Dear, Marilyn Jennings

Hey how are you doing? also how is the
family doing? I would also like to say
today 2-27-08 was the day I got found
guilty. I really didn't get a chance to
face the family & face Yall the way I
wanted to about what happen & to
Apologize so I would like to
Know will you & the family come
see me starday so I can get
something off my mind & say to
you & ~~the~~ family. Also I know
I will be down the road by
Monday. I would like to face
you so that I can tell you &
family it might be my last words
to yall. Im dont made that I
have life, I feel like I wasnt
trail fair, I feel like my life have
been took far as death.
Once again I would like to say
Im sorry to you & your son, and also
mother & father & family if so I
would be looking for you dis weeker

love you all

Mann

I'm surprised he actually had something else to say. He wanted me to come visit him. Was he for real? In his letter he stated that he had not had a fair trial. Reading that letter from him just made me mad. He was judged by 12 and my sister was carried by six. What about her justice? He wanted sympathy from me and I didn't have any. I didn't even entertain the thought of going to hear what he had to say. I had no time for that. I didn't want to see his face ever again and I was ready to move away so he wouldn't know my address.

change gon' come

November 26th, the day before Clara's birthday, Mom and Dad packed up their U-Haul and prepared to move back to South Carolina. Mom needed some fresh air - she had had enough of the city life. She wanted to go home where she could breathe and be with close family and friends. Dad wasn't working, so the only income would have would be from her, so she went back to live in her mother's house until they could save up some money and get a place of their own.

It hurt me to see her go, but it was the best thing for her and for me and my father. We needed to separate. I wasn't accepting any type of verbal abuse from him and he had no concern for the pain he was causing me. Mom wanted me to enjoy my life and she knew I couldn't if we all continued to live in the same house. It was a bittersweet moment, but I knew in my heart it was for the best. Days have turned into months and months will eventually become years without my sister being around. People say it will get easier, but I don't believe that. I still hope I will wake up and see that I was just having a bad dream. As time goes by, I miss her even more.

Her death has taught me so many things. I assumed that since we had all left home that we were safe from harm. I didn't realize that the things we had been exposed to had formed seeds within our beings that sprouted and spread to become dominant -overtaking part of our identity. We did the same things we saw done by our parents. We spoke the same language they did. I'm loud and bold like my father and can be a little mean. And if I am not paying attention, I curse worse than he does.

It is said that a family that prays together, stays together. Well, we didn't start off that way; but, through time, love, prayers, and lots of determination, we are now a family that prays together. We are definitely not perfect and still have a lot of brokenness that we need healing from, but we somehow manage to hold on to each other. Our lives have been rough but we continue to work on ways to become whole individuals, so that we can spread a different kind of love through our families. We all suffered a great loss and it has taken us all working toward the same goal to accept the things that we cannot change and embrace the things we can change. Being family again is what we work towards day by day, one step at a time, healing little by little.

My mother was 13 years old when she had me and 14 years old when she had my brother. She didn't have a close relationship with my biological father, so I didn't have the opportunity to grow up with him in my life. I remember meeting him once. I don't even remember his name. Mom only remembers his nickname. She feels somewhat ashamed at not being able to answer my questions concerning my biological father. This is a very hard subject for her to talk about, so I don't push the issue. She was so young when they met and my father was someone that was in town on a work assignment. He left as soon as it ended. Maybe one day I will meet him or be able to find out who he really was.

There were so many things I endured with my mother that most children probably wouldn't be able to forgive. The Bible teaches us in the book of Matthew, that God forgives us our debts, as we forgive our debtors. And "…lead us not into temptation, but deliver us from evil: For thine is the kingdom, and the power, and the glory…"Also, that when we forgive the wrong that has been done to us God will forgive us for the things that we do to other people. But if we do not have a forgiving heart, neither will God have one for us (Matthew 6:12-15).

My life experiences and the death of my sister have taught me in a painful way that when you think you are safe from harm you really are not. We must be careful for the things we expose ourselves to - especially for our children. We may not intend for our bad habits and lifestyles to be mimicked, but it happens. We are prone to adapt to our environment and become what we have been affected by. As time goes on, we branch out exploring different parts and paths of this world. The memories and behaviors we learn from our past are within us. We bring those bad habits to our new environment and spread the infection there. Until we recognize the damage this is causing and that we are destroying our generation, we will continue to destroy the future of our children, our family and our people.

We can no longer push domestic issues under the rug or bury them deep in our hearts hoping they just go away. In order to make sure that our future offspring are not cursed, we must peel back those layers of hurt and abuse and expose them for what they are and what they have done to us mentally and physically. Seek help if needed so that you can be healed and set free, and so that the things that haunted you fall behind you. We think that if we don't deal with things from our past that they will remain at rest, but little do we know that we bring those memories out through our attitudes, by the way we treat others, and the lifestyle we live: taking medication due to depression, not wanting to deal with the root of why we ended up this way. Then we wonder why our children have so many issues at such a young age. We can't explain their behavior and why they struggle so much to accept their identities.

Our children are what we created them to be. When we expose them to violence, drug abuse, depression, and emptiness we must understand that they will grow up with those same struggles. Until we stop being afraid of what others might say and admit within ourselves that there are some things we need to be delivered from, the devil will continue to destroy our families. We may not ever understand why we had to endure the things we endured in our lives, but know that there is a reason for it and if we survive it we can be a testimony for others that are going through trying to find a way out.

Chapter 14

THE WOMAN I AM TODAY

Broken, bitter, confused, mad, and angry about my past, I see only past beatings and endless whippings from my mother and father that I get angry about because it is a part of me. I am mad because of what happened to me and am angry because I didn't tell, nor did I fight back to stop it. I really think that would have made matters worse. But it hurts and the memories are still there. On top of that I now suffer with the loss of my little sister. I feel mistreated and I want somebody to pay for that. I am tired and I want to quit. I want to take a cord and beat my parents the way they beat me. I fight them in my mind. I cuss them out loud. I swing at the air as though they were there receiving my hits of pain. I cry because this is not how my life is supposed to be, but yet it is a part of me. People say that I am blessed. How so? I don't see it. I continue to have one turmoil after another. I am just mad. I didn't have a good childhood and I can't figure out how I am going to have a worthy adulthood. I am somehow determined to make my life the way I want it to be. I want to be so successful that my present and future overwhelm my past. I want new memories -- better ones, loving ones, complete ones, successful ones.

I get up and stand up first. I look in the mirror I tell myself that I am worthy of everything. I can do this. I am strong, I am smart, and I am ready. I wipe my face. I comb my hair. And I dress for success and step-by-step I start on my new journey. I am scared, I'm all alone, and yet I must carry on anyway. Why I do this, who knows? But I feel obligated to my brother -who messed up and is in prison-and to my sister - who has been robbed of the entirety of her destiny. So I must complete hers too. I also feel obligated to myself to see if it is really possible to fulfill a dream, to break a curse, and to start a new life for my offspring: my son and now my daughter. Yes, I am a single parent also. Am I so affected with my past that my children will suffer from my experiences? Will I inflict what was still in me on them? Have I kept so much hate inside me that I release it out on them? Were my parents trying to beat out my wisdom, my strength, my beauty, my self-confidence, my determination, my destiny and anything I ever dreamed of having? Did my parents try to embed in me hatred, misery, disappointment, low self-esteem, failure in my purpose? So I take the steps to find those missing parts of me. I need to know what my purpose is. What did I do to deserve such great pain? Am I being punished for something in my past or before my past? Was I here before and did wrong by God and this is my fate? It can't be, it just can't be.

Seven years have come and gone since that last time I saw Clara alive. Years of torment because she didn't have a headstone with her name on it. I waited patiently out of respect for Dad to purchase it for her, but due to some financial setbacks he was not able to get it. On Clara's grave there was a temporary brick that was very small that had her name on it, an Angel on both sides of it and a message that said "Beloved daughter, sister and a friend". It was a beautiful temporary marking until a permanent, more elaborate masterpiece replaced it. After a few monthly payments I was able to get her the tombstone that she deserved. I called Dad and told him that very same day and he thanked me. Within a few weeks I was called to come to the cemetery to look at the final draft before it was created and laid on Clara's grave. I arrived at the funeral home a little nervous. The lady that normally meet with me was not in that day. I told staff who I was and why I was there and they seem to be lost. I sat down in the waiting room while they located her file. I could hear them constantly saying Clara's name over and over and over. I felt disrespected. They acted as if she was just some file that they couldn't find. Did they forget that she was my sister?

Where was the compassion? I expected the staff to be more sympathetic when dealing with things of this nature. I could no longer hold back the tears. I began to cry in silence. I was getting upset and was about to get up and leave. The manager came out to assist me and to let me know that they were ready to show me the rough draft of Clara's tombstone. When the manager looked at me and saw that I was crying, she seem worried. I told her how uncomfortable I felt listen to them call Clara's name so many times. She sincerely apologized and gave me a hug. After several minutes of looking over the tombstone draft, I went home. The manager said that Clara's tombstone would be ready in four weeks. I immediately called my father and told him what I had done. He thanked me for helping him make his dream come true. I felt good and some weight was lifted off my heart knowing that this task was finally complete.

I felt renewed and ready to seek Christ more. The pain that I felt from issues of my past had moved on and I felt free. This life of mine was worth fighting for. I felt as though I could do all things through Christ that strengthens me. I felt God's presence in my life. He was listening to me and had been waiting for me to let Him in - all of Him. I was ready for a new beginning.

The house that I was living in didn't feel like where I needed to be. The time had come for me to move on as well - to relocate to a different area of town. I prayed first, asking God to guide me in the direction that I needed to go. Looking for the right house was not as easy as I thought it would be. I looked everywhere and nothing seem to fit me. I was getting frustrated and running out of time. Mom had come down to help pack up all my things in the house. Everyone was just waiting for me to tell me where we were going. I looked at at least fifteen houses from Union City to Ellenwood, Decatur, Lovejoy and McDonough. Finally, I got a call from a realtor who was returning my call about a house I was curious to see in Stockbridge. This house reminded me of the house I live in in Fairburn that Clara and I picked out. It was perfect. I filled out the application and was waiting for an answer to see if I was approved. The next day the people from the cemetery called that afternoon to tell me Clara's tombstone had arrive. I was happy that it came but upset because it reminded me where she was laid to rest. I missed her so much. I went to Clara's grave to see it. It was perfect. Standing there looking at her grave made me feel that I had just placed her body there a few day ago. I didn't stay long, the pain was too unbearable. I cried all the way home. I didn't feel like talking to anyone. That day was too overwhelming, so I decided to lay in bed and rest. Later that evening my phone rang and it was the realtor letting me know that I was approved and that we could start moving in the house in a few days. That was the best news I had all day. On April 1, 2014, I moved to Stockbridge, Georgia to begin my new journey - hoping to leave the past and some pain behind. My first few days in this new area of town were exciting to me. I took a deep breath and smiled as I drove around looking at all the things that GOD HAD BLESSED ME with. I felt a prosperous year ahead and was thankful for all of God's grace and mercy. We had just had another successful domestic violence walk. I met a lot of new people and was feeling positive knowing that we were bringing awareness to more people that would help us get the word out, but, most importantly, we were helping people to recognize the signs of domestic violence for themselves. I was ready to settle into my new home and plan out all the things I wanted to accomplish. I was feeling inspired, refreshed and renewed.

Just when I thought things were going great for me and that I had nothing to worry about, everything changed. July 14, 2014, I was driving to go pick up my uncle from work with my daughter in the back seat. I lost control of my vehicle and we hit a tree. I had to be airlifted to the hospital. I was told that I broke my hip, fractured my pelvis, broke my nose, and would need reconstructive surgery as the air bag had cracked some bones in my face. In order to do this surgery, I had to also endure a tracheotomy being put in my neck for me to continue breathing. I was in ICU and everyone was scared for my life. As I lay there, I asked myself, "How did I get to be in harm's way?" The doctors said I would need several surgeries, but there was a calm feeling in my spirit. And for the first time I didn't feel like I was in harm's way at all.

I felt like I was laying in the comfort of my Heavenly Father's arms. And He spoke to me saying, "I am here with you. I will never leave you nor forsake you." His rod and staff were there to comfort me. God's angels were there to assure me that all would be well throughout my surgery. God told me not to worry; He was going to make me better than I was before - inside and out.

Even though I was not able to talk, walk, or see, I felt at peace because of the anointing that I had over my life. The beating I had just taken was the enemy trying to disrupt God's plan, but God was there showing me who I was to Him and that no weapon formed against me was going to prosper. God had great plans for me, and He told me He was counting on me to be a testimony to others to lead them out of harm's way. So here I am, and here I stand. I am better than I was before because I know who I am and whose I am. Whatever the devil meant for bad in my life, God worked it out for my good. I am an overcomer and I will be victorious!

* * * * * * *

MOM

I love you and I forgive you for anything that I have held against you. I know you tried to raise me the best way you knew how. I learned so many things from you that I will cherish for the rest of my life. I know there were things that you also endured as a little girl that carried on into your married and the raising of us. You were a child yourself and you could have easily given me away but you didn't, and I thank you for that. I thank you for encouraging me to be a better person and to not settle for anything that was not fitting of the life I was seeking. Through our ability to talk as I grew older, we have been able to cry out our pains and hug through healing. You are my best friend and I would not change anything that I have experienced with you. My past has grown me to be the women I am today, so I forgive you and I thank you for it all.

I now ask you to forgive me for not understanding your pains and for the hatred I carried in my heart for years until I was able to forgive you. You have taught me how to be strong and independent. Your hard work and endurance is what kept this family together. You raised me to have morals and to make a difference in whatever

I do. The bond we have together is like no other and I am so grateful for you.

Words cannot describe the sacrifice you have made for us to be where we are today. Your heart is open wide for the world to have. I have always admired the love you give to others even when they don't give you that same love back. I work hard every day to have that same kind of love. Through these years you have had to face many storms. Some days I can see your weariness, and you just want to throw in the towel. Just remember God has his hands on you and he will continue to pull you through. Your endurance is beyond measure and your just rewards are well overdue. I look forward to making many more memories. As I continue to grow into the women that you have raised and what God has created, I embrace life's journey with a smile because I know no matter what I go through you will always be there, and am thankful.

Dad, wow, where do I begin? You hurt from so many things that, until you begin to trust God for everything that has happened in your life, you will never be able to be happy and enjoy your life. I know you are angry because you lost your mother at an early age and you barely know your father. You suffered a lot of abuse growing up and when you had children of your own, you inflicted that abuse onto us - almost destroying your blood line and your marriage. I hope that you can understand that God doesn't make any mistakes. Most importantly, remember John 3:16, "For God so loved the world that He gave His only begotten Son, that whosoever believeth in Him should not perish, but have everlasting life."

As you struggle to accept your second great loss, Clara (your mother being your first), I constantly pray that you give God a chance to renew your heart, mind, and soul. For many years, I have watched tears of hurt run down your face. It hurts me to see you hurting knowing that I can't do anything to fix it. Daddy, God can do all the impossible things that man can't do.

I forgive you for putting us in harm's way. I forgive you for nonsense beatings, for being the first man to call me a bitch, and whore, stupid, dumb and any of the derogatory names you repeatedly said to me most of my life. I want to also make peace with you for the domestic violence that I witnessed that damaged my mind and made it hard for me to believe that there was a better way to live. I also forgive you for your bad drinking habits and your drug abuse. I know you were mentally dealing with things beyond your control and you found drugs and alcohol to be the best way for you to deal with your life's struggle.

You have been in my life since I was three months old. Even though through the years you may have said things to me that you may regret, I know deep down that I am your daughter. I thank you for committing your life to me. You never left us nor turned your back on us. Thank you for always encouraging me to do better and to be a better person in life than you. You always felt like I was too good for any man and I thank you for that. Because of your harsh criticisms I have learned not to settle and not to let anyone mistreat me.

Over the years, we have come a long way in our communication and I love you for that. You taught me how to be a strong, independent, and determined leader and I hope I am making you proud. Since I was a little girl, you told me I was your right arm and I value that dearly. There are so many things that you and Mom were unable to do because you both started a family so early. I hope that I will be able to give you some of the things that you and Mom missed out on. You always said, "Change gon' come." Well Dad, God was listening. Change is on the way.

To my brother Thadd (who is currently in prison serving out his time): Come home, come home. I miss you so much that words cannot explain. Truth be told, I'm nervous. Will I ever see you again on this side of the bars? Will you make it out safely? Will I ever be able to show you where our sister lies? Can I wake up in the morning and see that you are there? I know it hurts you even more to not be able to be here with us as we learn to pick up the pieces of our lives without Clara.

I speak the blood of Jesus over your life and that no weapon formed against you shall prosper. I speak early release, and God's grace and mercy and favor so you can come home speedily. Your family needs you, your children need you, and I need you.

I am thankful…

* * * * * * * * * *

To God Almighty

For patiently waiting on me to get past the hurt I have been through, and to stop running from the very thing that You knew could heal me (and maybe heal a few others). Fear of what others might say was another reason it took me so long to write our story. Every time I heard Your voice I ignored it hoping you would pick someone else. I had so much doubt, brokenness, bitterness, and low self-esteem that I didn't think I was worthy of doing anything for Your glory. I am so thankful that You never let go. I can see clearly now. Heavenly Father, You showed me that if I just trust You that You will never leave me nor forsake me and that I will live a life of prosperity and righteousness.This journey has been rough. Writing this book has been very challenging. There were many times when I wanted to quit writing. I wanted to believe that it was just unreal for me to be writing this book and why even bother with it. Reliving some of my past pains was unbearable at times, but, God, You never let me go. You gave me the strength to press on, healing me along the way. I look at my life through Your Spirit and I thank you for it all. I am strong and able to assist others. I have my identity -- all of it -- and there is nothing the enemy can do to change it. My destiny has already been assigned by Your grace and mercy. I am here to carry it out. I am a living testimony for those who are trapped in the wilderness struggling to get out. Lord, I thank You for blessing me with this gift. I hope I have been obedient enough by giving You everything You have asked me to give concerning this book and every other area of my life.

I know this is just the beginning. With the anointing from God Almighty, I am victorious and I can do all things through Christ who strengthens me. I will continue to stand firm on Your Word and press on - breaking generational curses and helping other lost souls take back their destiny.

* * * * * * * * *

Pastor Gerry T Anderson

New Macedonia Baptist Church, Riverdale Georgia

Over seven years ago, I came to you and told you about the nightmares I was having and you told me to write them down, so I did. A couple of weeks later you asked me how my book was coming and I looked at you crazy. You told me I had a story to tell and it was time for me to write a book. I always felt as though God wanted me to write my life story but I just didn't believe I was worthy enough. When God used you to speak life to me and to give me confirmation, I pushed it away. You have always been a supportive and understanding pastor. I thank you for your leadership and for allowing God to use you to feed people like me. I can't thank you enough for all the things you have done in my life but I definitely thank God for having you as my pastor at the right and appointed time.

* * * * * * * * *

My sister clara:

When I look back over your life, I have to remember the day Mom was carrying you in her womb and she and Dad were fighting and he pushed her down a flight of stairs. Mom somehow was able to protect you from getting hurt while she suffered some minor injuries. You were born a healthy baby in spite of what could have been your ending. Your presence was known, you left your mark, and I am honored for the times we shared together. I thank God for the plans He had for you then. Even in your death you inspire me.

Writing this book was HARD. There were so many times when I just wanted to give up. The pain I feel only seems to get better when I write out our story. Losing you to domestic violence woke something up inside of me. Not being able to protect you has been the hardest thing Ihave ever had to face. I didn't see the signs of you being in any danger and I now know why. We grew up around so much domestic violence, but we never truly identified it for what it actually was. We were never educated on the definition of domestic violence, nor told what the signs were. It's sad to say, but I truly think we would not have paid the signs any attention unless they seemed to be extreme. That's the mistake we made. All signs of domestic violence are important. The warning signs are an opportunity for you to seek help and leave that current situation. As I find ways to live in this world without you, I promise to be your voice and fight to educate and help others see what we didn't see.

I think about you every single day. I am still trying to be strong, holding back my tears, and constantly praying my way through. I remember how you were dependent on me for direction and strength; I still feel your presence - needing me to continue being your big sister, helping other families through this walk that we have every year in your name honoring families who have lost someone the way I lost you. We, as a community, can show them that we care and I hope this will give them a little more strength and direction to carry on and want to fight with us to bring about this change.

About the Author, Marilyn Jennings:

Hailing from Atlanta, Georgia by way the small town of Estill South Carolina, I am the proud mom of a 16-year-old son and a 6 year old daughter who inspire me each day to do the advocacy work that is the source of this book. On April 3, 2007, I experienced the death of my younger sister Clara Riddles due to domestic violence.

As I struggled to accept the loss of the little sister I once believed God created just for me, whom I adored, nurtured and protected from domestic violence within our own home, I was grateful to seek healing through The National Young Ladies Coordinator of the Ladies of My Sister's Keeper/Atlanta Keepers organization. I went on to become the organization's Young Ladies National Coordinator, and in that capacity, I have helped every young lady mentee I encountered to embrace her true identity in order to fulfill her purpose and destiny and encourage her to pay it forward. This was also the training ground for me to become Clara's Voice through a series of community awareness walks and events.

I have led that Clara's Voice awareness event each year on the anniversary of her death to honor survivors, pay tribute to the victims and bring awareness loudly!I have alsopartnered with other domestic violence awareness groups such as Partnership Against Domestic Violence (PADV) and the Georgia Coalition Against Domestic Violence, going out into the community as motivational speaker, activist and advocate.

God has now steered me in the specific direction of creating the 501(3)(3) nonprofit organization, Harm's Way, Inc., with the first step of writing this book. "Harm's Way" reaches into the depths of my soul to share Clara's and my life story through devastating abuse and redemption, with the goal of encouraging change and breaking generational bondage while taking a stand toward my destiny.

I believe no matter how you start out in life, it does not determine how you will finish. I don't believe in riding with others on the "pity bus" but working toward the "Victory bus" because as long as I have faith and I believe, I can achieve all things. I say, <u>Live Your Best Life Now</u>--look forward not backward!

* * * * * * * * * *

**In loving memory
R.I.H. Clara Lee Riddles
November 27, 1984-April 3, 2007
#BetheVoice**